MORAL DISCERNMENT

Richard M. Gula, S.S.

PAULIST PRESS
New York / Mahwah, N.J.

ACKNOWLEDGMENTS

Excerpts from Robert Bolt, *A Man for All Seasons* (New York: Random House, Inc., Vintage Books © 1962) are used with permission of Random House, Inc.

Cover design by Cindy Dunne

Library of Congress Cataloging-in-Publication Data

Gula, Richard M.
    Moral discernment / Richard M. Gula.
        p. cm.
    Includes bibliographical references.
    ISBN 0-8091-3734-8 (alk. paper)
    1. Christian ethics—Catholic authors. 2. Conscience—Religious aspects—Catholic Church. 3. Decision-making (Ethics) 4. Catholic Church—Doctrines. I. Title.
BJ1249.G816   1997
241'.042—dc21   97-25298
                                                                          CIP

Published by Paulist Press
997 Macarthur Boulevard
Mahwah, New Jersey 07430

www.paulistpress.com

Printed and bound in the
United States of America

Contents

Introduction

"What should I do?" "How do I know if I have made the correct choice?" "Is this the right thing to do?" Each of us has asked these questions many times, whether in relation to complex issues of life and death (must we continue to treat Aunt Mary who is clearly dying?) or to simpler matters, such as deciding to read this book when other demands require our time. Because making moral decisions is a central part of our lives, this book proposes to help a critical adult audience interpret how conscience works in making a moral decision.

Over the past several years, I have frequently been asked to speak at religious education congresses for adults and at sabbatical programs for religious and clergy on the fundamentals of Christian moral living and on the process of making moral decisions. As the number of invitations to speak on the same topic increased, I began to ask each group what made this issue so popular. I have learned that it was due largely to the changes people had experienced in church, in society, and in culture that had made them bewildered about what's right and about how to go about discovering what they ought to do.

In the church, many have told me that they grew up in a very paternalistic ecclesial environment where they were not encouraged to think for themselves. In fact, some didn't even know that they were supposed to think! As one person put it, "We were told just to pray, pay, and obey." The paternalistic church was very directive. Bishops and priests were expected to have all the answers, were sought for answers, and generally gave answers to every practical moral question put to them. Now, people are trying to learn how to live in the church after the Second Vatican Council, which encouraged them to take responsibility for both discovering moral values and charting the direction of their lives.

Catholic theology today has recovered the insight that the moral wisdom of authoritative voices ought to enlighten conscience, not replace it. Now, people are expected to follow their conscience. Through its moral teaching the church helps us think more critically about our moral responsibilities and about what it means to be made in the image of God and called to be disciples of Jesus today. But many people aren't quite sure what all of that means: What is conscience? How do we form a conscience? What role does the teaching of the church play in all of this? How do we go about following conscience? What does discipleship look like? Everyone seems to know that, as disciples, we are called to be loving, but many do not know how to be guided by the love commandment. How do I know what love demands?

In society, many people have voiced a loss of confidence in the integrity and authority of our leaders. They are aware of ethical failures in high places and are suspicious of turning to those in authority for moral guidance. They feel that they have to learn how to make it on their own now but do not know how to go about this. Moreover, many have also voiced their experience of a morally disintegrating society. They name such things as the increase of drug use, violence, sexually transmitted diseases, divorce, political corruption, professional misconduct, fraud, greed, and ecological disasters. They ask, "Have we lost our moral compass?" They do not sense any consensus of values in society at large, and they feel that the high mobility of our society has created social fragmentation, which has undermined a stable network of support for their own values. They feel that they are being hurled about on the rough seas of moral confusion. They know that they must become self-consciously critical of the ways that they are making moral decisions, but they aren't sure how to go about it.

In culture, many feel that the rapid developments of science and technology are forcing new ethical dilemmas on us that we are not prepared to face. They give as examples the tough decisions that we have to make in health care brought on by the increased use of technology, together with the pressures of managed care to be cost-effective. They also name the ethical challenges posed by the pervasive presence of computer technology: pornography is now available on the Internet, for example, and e-mail may be monitored to detect fraud and other abuses. Others have detected a raising of a moral consciousness across the professions. We seldom pick up the papers or listen to the news without our attention being focused on ethics. With few institutions or professions having escaped scandal in recent years, most are responding by strengthening their training in ethics and by developing standards of conduct. There is an ethics committee in the House and Senate, institutional ethics committees in our hospitals, and departments of ethics in our professional schools; large corporations are hiring ethics consultants and providing ethics workshops for their employees. No one seems exempt anymore from ethical training and scrutiny.

The accelerated changes of this century in church, in society, and in culture mean an upheaval of values. Whenever change happens so rapidly around us, we are prone to take extreme positions. Either we cling to what is most familiar and so hold on for dear life to "traditional" values and the security of the way we were, or we throw all that out for the novelty of a new age. But "old" or "new," "traditional" or "modern," "conservative" or "progressive" are not the criteria for discerning the true, the right, and the good. In our world of contending values, where society offers a smorgasbord of options and where we can be just about anything we want to be, do just about anything we want to do, and indulge in just about any pleasure we wish, we need the skills of discernment so that we can test what is possible and retain what is good.

So the questions "What should I do?" and "How do I know I have made the correct choice?" and "Is this the right thing to do?" are increasingly more pressing. But they lead to few easy answers. Mark Twain is supposed to have said, "Religion is a dangerous thing, unless you get it right." The same can be said of morality, and it's hard to get it right, too. This book is written as an aid to adults who are trying to get it right.

This book is not catechetical in nature, and so it is not aimed at those who are still at the level of catechetical formation. Instead, this book presupposes some maturity in faith and an openness to explore questions concerning the nature of moral responsibility in a manner that honors the educational background presumed in most adult religious education programs, sabbatical programs, and theology courses.

While I focus on individual moral decision making, I am also concerned for the effect of these decisions on the common good. What one person decides shapes not only the individual but also the community. I believe that to strengthen the moral backbone of society, then, we would do well to focus on the individual's moral self-awareness. I am well aware that social structures limit and shape our thinking and our behavior, but individuals also shape social structures. Individual decisions have consequences that stretch far beyond the person deciding, as with the AIDS epidemic, for example, or terrorist bombing incidents or oil spills. The decision of one person affects the many. The shape of society crystallizes around decisions made at the personal level.

To introduce an adult community to the fundamentals of making a moral decision from a Catholic perspective, I have structured this book in three parts. Part I, "Foundations," is about the nature of the moral conscience and practical reasoning. Here I make the ever-important distinction between conscience in the psychological sense of the superego and the moral conscience as it has been understood in the theological tradition. In the first chapter I develop the notion that conscience is not the teacher of moral doctrine, but the practical judgment of what one is to do. Conscience, in its proper moral sense, is the judgment of practical reasoning by which one decides to do what is right and to avoid what is wrong. Then I show that conscience is not a law unto itself, but must be formed in community by appealing to sources of moral wisdom. I conclude with a brief description of the three requirements for a person to be able to act in conscience—knowledge, freedom, and emotions.

In the second chapter I give a fuller treatment of practical moral reasoning, or, as I perfer to call it, the process of moral discernment. Traditionally, this is what we would call practicing "prudence." I first identify the need for moral reflection, and then distinguish moral discernment from other forms of moral reasoning.

Part II, "Moral Discernment," is the core of this book. There I take a slow walk through the three spheres of influence on the process of discernment—the social, situational and personal contexts.

Part III, "Application," rounds out my treatment of discernment by moving into the pastoral domain of giving moral guidance. In this last part, I distinguish between the task of moral theology and that of pastoral moral guidance. I then offer a "survivor's guide" for trying to provide moral guidance in the midst of moral and theological pluralism. I conclude with a model of pastoral moral guidance and illustrate it with the dialogue of a case consultation with a pastoral care minister regarding moral guidance on a health care decision about whether to treat or not to treat.

I have included with each chapter some questions I have found helpful for guiding discussion with adults on this material. These questions have also proved to aid their understanding and use of this material.

The beginning of each chapter poses a few questions to explore one's **Present Understanding.** The goal of this first step is to have the participants make a brief statement of their feelings, understanding, or way of acting toward the issue about to be discussed. This will enable them to put their own experience in dialogue with what I have to say in the chapter.

At the end of each chapter are two more movements in the pedagogical process. The first is **Critical Reflection.** This step aims to affirm the participants in some aspect of their present understanding of the topic at hand. It also invites them to broaden their awareness with a new insight and to raise new questions about the issue. The last movement is **Appropriation.** It invites them to rediscover how the theme under consideration is already at work in their lives. It also challenges them to make some adjustments to their behavior in the future.

The book is especially designed for those who are interested in the fundamentals of making moral decisions but who do not have the time or skill to probe primary sources. While I have drawn heavily on scholarly works, I have not tried to make this book another scholarly treatment of conscience in its theological roots. Nor have I tried to spell out the theories of cognitive psychology or of philosophy that underlie my model of discernment. Those who will be looking for these presuppositions and a defense of them will be disappointed. I am only trying to provide a reasonable synthesis for those who are somewhat mature in their faith and whose background does not include the academic study of moral theology, but who want to think critically about what takes place when a responsible, adult Christian believer acts in conscience. To put it briefly, this book is meant to contribute to the process of being trained in prudence—the virtue of making responsible decisions.

I have kept references and quotations to a minimum so as to keep the book to a manageable size and to make it readable and engaging for adults. What cannot be acknowledged in these few notes and references is my indebtedness to the students in my classes and to the participants in many adult and clergy education sessions who shared openly their experiences and frustrations and who asked many probing questions, which I have used to focus this book. A special word of thanks goes to my Sulpician colleagues Frs. Philip S. Keane, S.S., Thomas R. Ulshafer, S.S., and Ronald D. Witherup, S.S., for their help in refining the manuscript. I am also grateful to the comments and contributions of Mrs. Elizabeth Lilly, Mrs. Marilyn Neri, and Sr. Joan Marie O'Donnell, R.S.M., who read the manuscript with the interest of the adult audience for which it is intended. A word of thanks also goes to Fr. Stephen C. Rowan of the Archdiocese of Seattle and Seattle University, who patiently read the manuscript and offered many helpful suggestions to make it clearer.

I. Foundations

1. Conscience

PRESENT UNDERSTANDING:

- *What do you understand by the moral conscience?*
- *How do you form your conscience?*
- *When do you consider yourself to be acting in conscience?*

☛

"Let conscience be your guide" is a reliable moral maxim. But what does it mean and what does it demand of us? Conscience is a difficult notion to understand; it is even more difficult to explain how it operates. Like the elusive butterfly, it evades being captured by brusque and clumsy methods.

Yet we all know that we have a conscience, even if we can't explain how we got it or how it works. We know that we stand for certain things, we struggle over deciding what to do, and we feel pangs of conscience when we do something wrong, even something petty like taking cookies from the cookie jar. Questions of conscience arise regularly and not just over the big issues like taking a stand on war, on crime and punishment, on health care reform, or on affirmative action policies. Questions of conscience also arise on very personal matters like whether to blow the whistle on a coworker who is doing a sloppy job, or whether to reveal a brother's alcoholism to his fiancée, or whether to take more time away from the family to play another round of golf. If we are ever going to grow in our loving relationship with God and neighbor, then we need to discern what is truly loving. Conscience is our capacity for making such a discernment.

The first task in this book is to clarify what is meant by conscience so that we can appreciate how it relates to the larger process of making moral decisions. I will first distinguish the moral conscience from what it is not—its psychological cousin, the superego. Then I will sketch in greater detail the meaning of conscience in the moral tradition by giving particular attention to the formation of conscience, the relation of conscience to character and choice, the goal of a mature conscience, and the requirements for acting in conscience.

Conscience/Superego Mix-up

The moral conscience must be distinguished from what it is not. Time and again I have found that adult audiences experience liberation when they are able to distinguish the moral conscience from what some psychologists mean by the superego. Psychologists of the Freudian school tell us that we have three structures to our personality: The *id*—that unconscious reservoir of instinctual drives largely dominated by the pleasure principle; the *ego*—the conscious structure that operates on the reality principle to mediate the forces of the id, the demands of society, and the reality of the physical world; and the *superego*—the ego of another superimposed on our own to serve as an internal censor to regulate our conduct by using guilt as its powerful weapon.[1]

To understand the superego, we need to begin with childhood. As we develop through childhood, the need to be loved and approved is our basic need and drive. We fear punishment as children, not for its physical pain only, but more because it represents a withdrawal of love. So we regulate our behavior so as not to lose love and approval. As a matter of self-protection, we absorb the standards and regulations of our parents or anyone who has authority over us. The authority figure takes up a place within us to become a kind of psychic parent or police officer keeping an eye on our behavior and giving us commands and setting out prohibitions. Since we carry this authority with us in the unconscious structure of our mind, the voice of this authority is always and everywhere present to us. It tells us that we are good when we do what we have been told to do, and it tells us that we are bad and makes us feel guilty when we do not do what we should.

I once had a very clear experience of the superego at work when I took my three-year-old niece for a walk through her neighborhood. We were chatting about whatever it is one chats with a three-year-old about when we came to the corner with a traffic light. She interrupted our conversation with "Look both ways before crossing the street." That had nothing to do with our conversation, so I asked her where it came from. She said, "That's Mom talking." Now Mom was still back at the house! This command, which she had heard before when her mom took her for a walk, was now inside her as a means of social and self-control. That is the way the superego is formed and how it works. At this stage in the life of a three-year-old, the external voice of authority, her mom, is in the process of becoming an internal voice of authority. For now, she obeys the command because of the authority her mom has over her, not because she has appropriated the value of safety enshrined in the command. Conscience in the sense of superego represents constraint. It is the internalized mechanism to regulate behavior so as to avoid punishment and buy safety. It acts out of the fear of punishment and the need for acceptance.

The superego is like a tape playing in our heads all the shoulds and have-tos that we heard in the process of growing up under the influence of authority figures. A simplified way of thinking about the difference between superego and moral conscience is to distinguish between shoulds or have-tos and wants as the source of the commands directing our behavior. Shoulds and have-tos belong to someone else. The wants of conscience (what the truest self would want to do) belong to us. A friend of mine once reminded me, "Don't 'should' on me. I don't want to be the way you think I should be." She had it exactly right.

Perhaps we can better appreciate the difference between conscience and superego by identifying some outstanding contrasting features. Whereas the shoulds and have-tos of the superego look to authority, the wants of conscience look to personalized and internalized values, or acquired virtues. The superego acts merely out of the obligation to be obedient. The moral conscience, by contrast, exercises responsible freedom— the freedom of wanting to do what we ought to do as virtuous persons because we own the values that we are expressing. When we act out of the fear of losing love or out of our need to be accepted and approved, the superego is at work. The moral conscience, on the other hand, acts out of love for others and in response to the call to commit ourselves to value. The conscience/superego mix-up helps us understand in part what makes a person with an overly developed or overly active superego have a difficult time distinguishing between what God is calling him or her to do from what someone else in authority (like Mom) says he or she should do.

John W. Glaser gives a more sophisticated contrast of the differences between superego and moral conscience in his still-valuable article, "Conscience and Superego: A Key Distinction."[2] In the accompanying chart, I have reconstructed Glaser's nine contrasting characteristics of the superego and moral conscience. This listing is not intended to be exhaustive. I have added emphasis to the points of contrast in Glaser's list, and I have slightly reworded his characteristics to bring his language into line with what I am using here.

Although basically a principle of censorship and control, the superego still has a positive and meaningful function in our personalities. In children, the superego is a primitive but necessary stage on the way to a true moral conscience. In adults, the

SUPEREGO	**CONSCIENCE**
1. *Commands* us to act for the sake of gaining approval or out of fear of losing love.	1. *Responds to an invitation* to love; in the very act of responding to others, one cocreates self-value.
2. *Turned in toward self* in order to secure one's sense of being of value, of being lovable.	2. *Fundamental openness* that is oriented toward the other and the value that calls for action.
3. Tends to be *static* by merely repeating a prior command. Unable to learn or function creatively in a new situation.	3. Tends to be *dynamic* by a sensitivity to the demand of values that call for new ways of responding.
4. Oriented primarily *toward authority:* not a matter of responding to value but of obeying the command of authority blindly.	4. Oriented primarily *toward value:* responds to the value that deserves preference regardless of whether authority recognizes it or not.
5. Primary attention is given to *individual acts* as being important in themselves apart from the larger context or pattern of actions.	5. Primary attention is given to the *larger process* or *pattern.* Individual acts become important within this larger context.
6. Oriented toward the *past:* "The way we were."	6. Oriented toward the *future:* "The person one ought to become."
7. *Punishment* is the sure guarantee of reconciliation. The more severe the punishment, the more certain one is of being reconciled.	7. Reparation comes through *structuring the future* toward the value in question. Creating the future makes good the past.
8. The transition from *guilt to self-renewal* comes fairly easily and rapidly by means of confessing to the authority.	8. *Self-renewal* is a gradual process of growth that characterizes all dimensions of development.
9. Often finds a *great disproportion* between feelings of guilt experienced and the value at stake, for extent of guilt depends more on the significance of authority figure disobeyed than the weight of the value at stake.	9. Experience of *guilt is proportionate* to the degree of one's knowledge, freedom, and emotional stability as well as the value at stake, even though the authority may never have addressed the specific value.

superego is an internalized moral legacy from our unconscious past. It functions positively when integrated into a mature conscience to relieve us from having to decide freshly in every instance those matters that are already legitimately determined by convention or custom. The difference between the working of the superego in the child and the adult is one of degree and not of kind. In concrete cases, the superego and moral conscience do not exist as pure alternatives in undiluted form. We experience them as a mixture in our efforts to decide what to do. But to be able to say that we are acting in conscience, there must be a greater influence of the internalized values that we own over the superego and the pull of social pressure to conform.

I hope that the chart on p. 15 is sufficient to clear up the confusion between superego and the moral conscience. Now I want to offer an interpretation of what our theological tradition means by the moral conscience.

The Moral Conscience

Achieving clarity about the moral conscience has been complicated by the way the theological tradition has spoken of it.[3] What we understand today by conscience is rooted in the biblical notion of the heart. The heart is the seat of vital decisions, for it is the center of feeling and reason, decision and action, intention and consciousness.[4] The hope of the messianic prophecies is for the people to receive a new heart so that their inmost inclinations will be to live out the gift of divine love that they receive in the covenant (Jer 31:31–34; Ez 11:14–21).

In the New Testament, Jesus reflects the Hebrew understanding that the unity of the person is centered in the heart. From a person's heart come the evil ideas that lead one to do immoral things (Mk 7:21), whereas a good person produces good from the goodness in the heart (Lk 6:45). Paul is the chief New Testament author to speak of conscience. He weaves together Hebrew and Greek thought to identify conscience as our fundamental awareness of the difference between good and evil, as a guide to loving decisions, and as a judge of actions unbecoming a Christian (Rom 2:15; 1 Tm 1). From the biblical vision of the heart as that dimension of us most sensitive and open to others, especially to God's love or grace, we can develop our theological understanding of conscience.

The medieval debates spoke of conscience as a function of the intellect (practical reasoning) or of the will (choosing). The post-Tridentine era made it a rationalistic operation that functioned in a deductive way from first principles. The Second Vatican Council's document *The Church in the Modern World* opened us to a new era of reflecting on the nature of conscience when it taught:

> In the depths of his conscience, man detects a law which he does not impose upon himself, but which holds him to obedience. Always summoning him to love good and avoid evil, the voice of conscience can when necessary speak to his heart more specifically; do this, shun that. For man has in his heart a law written by God. To obey it is the very dignity of man; according to it he will be judged. Conscience is the most secret core and sanctuary of a man. There he is alone with God, whose voice echoes in his depths. (*GS,* n. 16)

On the inviolability of conscience, the *Declaration on Religious Freedom* teaches:

> In all his activity a man is bound to follow his conscience faithfully, in order that he may come to God, for whom he was created. It follows that he is not to be forced to act in a manner contrary to his conscience. Nor, on the other hand is he to be restrained from acting in accordance with his conscience, especially in matters religious. (*DH,* n. 3)

More recently, Pope John Paul II, in his encyclical on moral theology, *Veritatis Splendor,* affirms conscience as the link between human freedom and moral truth when he says that the

relationship between freedom and God's law "is most deeply
lived out in the 'heart' of the person, in his moral conscience"
(*VS,* n. 54).

We can distill the wisdom of the tradition on conscience for
our contemporary understanding of it by distinguishing three
dimensions of conscience: a *capacity,* a *process,* and a *judgment.*
As a capacity, conscience is our fundamental ability to discern
good and evil. Except for those who are seriously brain damaged
or emotionally traumatized, everyone seems to have this raw
capacity as part of our human nature. Conscience has also been
used to name the process of discovering what makes for being a
good person and what particular action is morally right or wrong.
This is the dimension of conscience that is subject to being formed
and informed through experience and critical investigation of the
sources of moral wisdom. This inquiry yields the actual judgment
that concludes, "This is what I must do because this is what moral
truth demands." This is the practical judgment that takes place in
one's heart where we are alone with God. As *Veritatis Splendor*
puts it, "It is the judgment which applies to a concrete situation the
rational conviction that one must love and do good and avoid evil"
(*VS,* n. 59). This is the judgment that fulfills the maxim, let conscience be your guide. The guidance this judgment gives us will be
as reliable as the efforts we make to inform it.

In light of these three dimensions of conscience, a contemporary approach to conscience focuses on the whole person.
Conscience includes not only cognitive and volitional aspects but
also affective, intuitive, and somatic ones as well. We understand
the moral conscience holistically as an expression of the whole
self as a thinking, feeling, intuiting, and willing person. *Conscience is the whole person's commitment to value and the judgment one makes in light of that commitment of who one ought to
be and what one ought to do or not do.*

Many people still mistake the appeal to conscience as a
stand for individual freedom and against authority. In short, they

think conscience is a freedom from authority. This notion could not be further from the truth. Conscience is not a law unto itself, nor is it the teacher of moral doctrine. To invoke conscience means to be subject to moral truth and to make a practical judgment of what to do in light of that truth. The freedom of conscience is the freedom to act in truth.

Traditionally, we spoke of the judgment of conscience as the "proximate norm of personal morality." This does *not* mean that conscience independently determines what is good and what is evil. Nor does it mean that conscience makes all morality relative to a person's own desires or that one's moral judgment is true merely by the fact that the judgment comes from one's conscience. It does mean that the person's sincerely reflective judgment of what to do sets the boundary for acting with integrity, or sincerity of heart. To say, "My conscience tells me" means, "I may be wrong, but I understand this to be an objective demand of morality and so I must live by it lest I turn from the truth and betray my truest self."

My favorite illustration of conscience at work is Sir Thomas More, as portrayed by author Robert Bolt in *A Man for All Seasons*. This play can be read as a study of the conflicts that arise between one who answers to conscience and those who choose to follow what is convenient. Thomas More faces up to the demands of his conscience over the prestige of his service to the king. In so doing, he creates a conflict between what is expedient or popular and what he holds so strongly that it is inseparable from his very self. More knows that choices are self-determining. When we choose one course of action over another, we make ourselves into certain kinds of persons. What we do under difficult conditions reveals who we are and what we are like more than does what we do in "normal" times.

The following scene takes place in the jail cell when Thomas More's daughter, Margaret, comes to persuade him to swear to the Act of Succession.

MORE: You want me to swear to the Act of Succession?

MARGARET: "God more regards the thoughts of the heart than the words of the mouth." Or so you've always told me.

MORE: Yes.

MARGARET: Then say the words of the oath and in your heart think otherwise.

MORE: What is an oath then but words we say to God?

MARGARET: That's very neat.

MORE: Do you mean, it isn't true?

MARGARET: No, it's true.

MORE: Then it's a poor argument to call it "neat," Meg. When a man takes an oath, Meg, he's holding his own self in his own hands. Like water. *(He cups his hands)* And if he opens his fingers *then*—he needn't hope to find himself again. Some men aren't capable of this, but I'd be loath to think your father one of them.[5]

The scene emphasizes that any choice that really involves an act of conscience includes one's whole self with it. Thomas More shows that, when we do not act according to conscience, our very self can be lost. Acts of conscience are fundamentally acts of integrity.

To follow one's conscience as Thomas More did is answering to the call of God one hears from within the depths of one's own person. If one truly believes in his or her heart (i.e., with one's whole self) that this line of action rather than another is God's objective call, then that line of action is no longer simply one option among many. It becomes the morally required line of action that one must take. In a sense, we feel within us that we really have no other choice. This is the sense of Martin Luther's "Here I stand, I can do no other." Not only Luther, but others too have fearlessly stood up before tyranny and declared, "I cannot, will not be moved." This is what we mean by saying that a person is "bound in conscience."

We give primacy to conscience and regard the moral claims of conscience as absolutely binding because in conscience we meet God's Spirit leading us. As *Veritatis Splendor* affirms, conscience does not command things on its own authority, as though the person were in dialogue with him or herself. But the command of conscience, "Do this, shun that," comes ultimately from God's authority (*VS,* n. 58). Conscience is the place where God speaks to us. Thus, obeying conscience is giving witness to God. To transgress the command of conscience would be to act contrary to what we believe God is calling us to do in a specific instance.

The Formation of Conscience

The obligation to follow conscience presupposes that we have properly formed our conscience. This is a function of the second dimension of conscience named above, that is, conscience as a process of discernment. This is the process of a continual conversion to what is true and good, the search for who we ought to be and for what we ought to do in faithful response to God's call. We are morally good to the extent that we honestly try to discover what is right. We are bad if we fail to try. But trying to find out what is right is different from actually attaining it. Forming conscience is a lifelong task and an ongoing process of conversion.

Every conscience is social. That is to say, convictions of conscience are shaped, and moral obligations are learned, within the communities that influence us. While the judgment of conscience is always made *for* oneself (what I must do), it is never formed *by* oneself. No one can ever identify moral truth entirely on one's own. We are too limited by experience and knowledge or almost blind from being accustomed to sin to recognize moral truth all by ourselves. So we must always take counsel before acting in conscience. That means that we ought to consult the established sources of wisdom.

As *humans* we consult our own experience as well as the experience of family, friends, colleagues, and experts in the field that pertains to our area of judgment at hand. We analyze and test the stories, images, laws, rituals, actions, and norms by which the various communities in which we participate live the moral life.

As *Christians* we turn to the testimony of scripture, especially the words and deeds of Jesus, the religious convictions of our creeds, the lives of moral virtuosos, and the informed judgment of theologians past and present who help interpret the traditions of Christian life.

As *Catholics* we pay attention to our rich heritage of stories, images, devotional practices, and spiritual disciplines. But we are also to attend to the truth in the moral instruction of the magisterium, the teaching office of the pope and of the bishops. The magisterium is charged with the mission of understanding, interpreting, and applying the moral truth found in revelation and natural law to issues facing us. This teaching office—guided by the promise of the Spirit—carries a weight and presumption of truth for Catholics that no other teacher can rightfully claim. The moral guidance of the magisterium helps us check the bias of our own sinfulness, and it expands our moral awareness of how we can keep the gospel alive from age to age. Since our consciences must be formed in accord with moral truth and in the light of Christ, Catholics must include this privileged source of moral guidance in making moral choices.

Conscience and Character

The proper formation of conscience uses these sources of moral wisdom not only to answer the practical moral question, "What ought I to do?" but also the prior moral question, "What sort of person ought I to become?" The aim of forming conscience is not simply to inquire about the right thing to do by gathering information and thinking it over; it must also include the fuller development of a person's moral character: one's attitudes, motives, intentions, affections, and perspective. The moral life is a matter of who we are as well as what and how we choose.

To appreciate what the fuller formation of conscience requires, we might consider the goal toward which we are striving in forming conscience. I think this anecdote expresses it well:

> When I was seven I had to have my tonsils removed. The operation was scheduled for early in the morning, and I was forbidden to have any food or drink after dinner the evening before. The operation was delayed, and I recall lying for several hours on a surgical bed in a corridor outside the operating room. My mouth was so dry that I couldn't swallow. My lips were so parched they hurt.
>
> There I was, a child all alone, sobbing and begging for a glass of water. Every now and then a nurse passed by, saw me crying, explained why I couldn't have a drink, and went back to work. Then one nurse I had not seen before stopped and asked if she could help. Again I pleaded for water. Like the others, she explained that she couldn't give me anything to drink, but then she did something totally unexpected: She told me that her lips were moist with lipstick and that maybe a kiss would make my lips moist, too. She bent down, kissed me, wished me well, and went back to her work.[6]

Where did this Good Samaritan nurse get the courage to stay and not run away from another complaining kid? Where did she get the practical wisdom to know that moist lips kissing parched lips was the right thing to do? No code of ethics for nurses prescribes this as a professional requirement. What goes into forming conscience that produces such empathic, right behavior?

Moral character such as this nurse exhibited emerges not from agreeing to arguments but from forming habits. Habits reflect the beliefs, ideals, and images of life that we receive from the communities in which we live, especially the people who have fascinated us enough to capture our imaginations. Maybe if we were disembodied spirits, arguments and abstract analysis would work. But we are embodied persons who learn through experience most of all. So we need to begin with people of good character, like Aunt Rose and Uncle Pat. The power of example is the most formative influence on shaping character. We become persons of good character by acting in the same spirit that persons of good character act.

The fuller formation of conscience, then, must pay attention not only to the rules of explicit moral instruction, but also to the communities that influence us, the images and beliefs these communities reinforce, and the people who embody a community's style of life in a way that captivates us so that we would want to be like them. In the end, the decisions we make and the actions we take will reflect the kind of character we develop and the situation in which we find ourselves. What we do ultimately reveals and shapes our character.

Conscience and Choice

Even though the moral conscience is subject to truth, is oriented to moral values, and is committed to doing what is right and to avoiding what is wrong, conscience can still err. For example, in the process of forming conscience, our sinfulness can so blind us that we miss or distort some of the facts of the case. As a result, we would be mistaken in our judgment about the right thing to do. Or we may get the facts straight but misjudge what best respects human dignity and serves the well-being of persons. Then we would be acting from an erroneous conscience and not merely from an error of fact.

For example, consider the parent who confronts a child with tough love when everyone else can see that support is most needed at the moment. We call this acting with an erroneous conscience. Or take the well-known story from *The Adventures of Huckleberry Finn* where Mark Twain describes how Huck could not bring himself to turn in Jim, the runaway slave. According to the mind of a

Missouri boy of the 1840s, Huck Finn's conscience was erroneous, even though sincere and properly formed according to the civil and church teaching of the time. Huck believed that he was doing wrong by not betraying Jim. But did he really do the wrong thing? Today we would say that he did the right thing but that his analysis of his behavior was mistaken. In his mind, he acted sincerely but mistakenly. This shows that, even when sincere in wanting to do right, we can still miss what is truly good objectively.

The dignity and inviolability of conscience do not exempt us from making mistakes. Acting with an erroneous conscience can lead one to do what is wrong (as in the case of the parent) or to do what is right but think that it is wrong (as in the case of Huck Finn). But acting with an erroneous conscience does not necessarily make one a bad person. Pope John Paul II's encyclical *Veritatis Splendor* follows a long-standing tradition when it speaks of the erroneous conscience as possibly resulting from invincible ignorance, that is, the person acting is unaware of being wrong and is unable to overcome this ignorance on his or her own. A person who does wrong as a result of invincible ignorance commits a nonculpable error of judgment. This error does not make what is wrong become right, but neither does the error compromise the dignity of conscience (*VS,* n. 62).

The dignity of conscience ensures that the one who makes a sincere effort to inform conscience and then lives by it will not betray his or her integrity. It does not guarantee that one will discern what is truly good. No one can be blamed for doing something wrong if he or she sincerely tried to find out what is right. If a person acts on the basis of a nonculpable error of judgment, then that person cannot be held culpable for it. We say that that person did the best he or she knew how to do. It is those who don't even try to find out what is right that we need to worry about. As the encyclical explains, conscience compromises its dignity when it is "culpably erroneous," that is, when we show little concern for seeking what is true and good (*VS,* n. 63). Otherwise, we must

always follow the light of our conscience in good faith and leave
the rest to God. We believe that God will judge us, not on the basis
of our actions being objectively right or wrong, but on the basis of
the sincerity of our hearts in seeking to know and to do what is
right, even if we make a mistake. But anyone who acts against
one's conscience is always culpable, even though nothing objectively wrong is done. Why? Because the judgment of conscience
always speaks in the name of that truth about the good that we are
called to seek sincerely, even if we might be off the mark through
invincible ignorance (cf. *VS,* nn. 60–63).

Generally, at this point in presenting this material, someone
usually interjects the question that if a person who follows one's
conscience is not necessarily a bad person, then can we say that a
serial killer, or someone like Hitler, is not bad because he was following his conscience? This question forgets that to say that one is
acting in conscience, even the erroneous conscience, presumes the
sincere effort to find out what is right. Can we really say that a person who takes on the way of life of planned killing is seriously trying to find out what is right? The enormity of such evil suggests
otherwise. The problem is really that such a person was acting without a conscience. Moreover, even if such a person were acting in
"good" conscience, we would still have the right to intervene to stop
the actions because of the seriousness of the evil being done. One
may act in conscience but still do what is objectively wrong. As persons who may be negatively affected by others' conscientious acts,
we cannot simply condone their actions because they come from a
judgment of conscience. Some actions must be restrained, especially when they would inflict grave risk or harm on others.

The Goal: A Mature Conscience

A person with a mature conscience takes responsibility for
his or her own formation and judgment before God. Although in
dialogue with the various sources of moral wisdom, the mature

conscience ultimately decides for itself. It does not surrender its soul to another and abdicate responsibility. Martin Buber's tale of Rabbi Zusya succinctly illustrates that the integrity of conscience requires being true to one's self. Out of our loyalty to conscience we will witness to God and be judged by God.

> The Rabbi Zusya said a short time before his death, "In the world to come, I shall not be asked, 'Why were you not Moses?' Instead, I shall be asked, 'Why were you not Zusya?'"[7]

If a person spends a lifetime doing what he or she is told to do by someone in authority simply because the authority says so or because that is the kind of behavior expected by the group, then that person never really makes moral decisions that are his or her own. For moral maturity one must be one's own person. It is not enough merely to do what one has been told simply because an authority commands it. The morally mature person must be able to perceive, choose, and identify oneself with what one does. In short, we build stronger character and give our lives meaning by committing our freedom, not by abdicating it to someone in authority. We cannot claim to be virtuous, to have strong moral character, or to give direction to our lives if we act simply on the basis that we have been told to do such and such. As long as we do not direct our own activity, we are not yet free, morally mature persons.

Who Can Act in Conscience?

This note on moral maturity leads us to ask, then, "Who can make moral decisions of conscience?" If conscience is the whole person's commitment to value, then to act in conscience requires some degree of knowledge, freedom, and affective capacity to care for others and to commit oneself to moral values.

Knowledge

The kind of knowledge required to act in conscience obviously includes the capacity to reason, that is, to reflect, to analyze, or to think in a somewhat critical fashion. But knowledge for acting in conscience also requires an appreciation of moral values, especially the value of persons and what contributes to their well-being. We call this heartfelt grasp of the quality of persons and events *evaluative knowledge,* in contrast to *conceptual knowledge,* which is merely awareness of facts, rules, and values. Without a heartfelt understanding of values but with merely conceptual knowledge about them, we act more out of hearsay than conviction. To reach an appreciation of values requires experience and reflection, not just right information.

But even more than these kinds of knowledge, those who act in conscience also need to be self-reflective and to have reached some degree of self-awareness that puts them in touch with what is going on inside them. For this reason, it is not surprising to discover that the greatest obstacle to good decision making is a lack of self-awareness. The key to acting in conscience is to be self-conscious.

Since right moral living involves living according to the capacities we have, becoming aware of one's self is the cornerstone of moral, spiritual, and psychological growth. Knowledge of the self includes knowing not only one's limits but also one's strengths, potentials, and preferences. We are morally required to live within the capacities we have; no one is morally obligated to do what he or she is incapable of doing. So we would do well to know our limits and our capacities. We only frustrate ourselves morally when we try to run ahead of our graces, that is, when we try to live beyond our means. We incur guilt unnecessarily if we compare our moral efforts with those of someone with a capacity different from our own. We need to learn, then, the limits and potentials that are ours.

A basic demand of Christian morality is to live according to the graces we have received. The goal of moral striving is to become what God has made us to be by expressing ourselves within the limits of our natural endowment. In this way we live out of our blessings and give thanks and praise to God by using well what is ours. Living in this way makes the moral life a continuous expression of praise and thanksgiving to God, who has endowed us with different gifts and with different degrees of the same gifts.

But who among us can say that we have attained a deep level of self-knowledge? We are all on the way to a clearer awareness of who we are. If we do not have a full or clear grasp of who we are, how much more difficult it is to have a total, explicit grasp of someone else's true moral self. We have no window into another person's soul that would allow us to see clearly enough where she or he stands before God. Sir Thomas More demonstrates that the judgment of conscience extends to no one but oneself.

> NORFOLK: I'm not a scholar, as master Cromwell [the prosecutor] never tires of pointing out, and frankly I don't know whether the [King's] marriage was lawful or not. But damn it, Thomas, look at those names.... You know those men! Can't you do what I did, and come with us, for fellowship?
>
> MORE: *(moved)* And when we stand before God, and you are sent to Paradise for doing according to your conscience, and I am damned for not doing according to mine, will you come with me, for fellowship?
>
> CRANMER: So those of us whose names are there are damned, Sir Thomas?
>
> MORE: I don't know, Your Grace. I have no window to look into another man's conscience. I condemn no one.[8]

As the witness of Thomas More so ably demonstrates, we ought to refrain from making any moral judgments of condemnation of another, even if their observable patterns of behavior are destructive of human well-being.

Freedom

To act in conscience one must also be able to direct one's actions according to self-chosen goals. Actions that are not under our control cannot really be considered within the realm of conscience. For example, we cannot be held responsible for a tree falling on our house in a windstorm. Such an act of nature is beyond our control. But we can be held responsible for how we respond to the destruction it brings.

In our pastoral tradition, we have recognized limits to responsibility. That I *ought* to do something implies that I *can* do it. It is unreasonable to demand that someone do what is beyond his or her capacity of knowledge, freedom, and emotional or moral strength. We need to keep this in mind when acting pastorally toward a person. The final chapter on pastoral moral guidance will show how we must respect the limited capacity of a person and not impose what a person is incapable of doing.

Our basic freedom is the freedom to make someone of ourselves. As Christians we direct our basic freedom toward becoming one with God. But since we experience God and express our relationship to God in mediated ways, our basic freedom of self-determination gets expressed through the particular choices that we make in life. (We also call this free will.) Our freedom to choose must be exercised across a broad spectrum of possibilities but within the limits of nature and nurture. What we do is at least partially up to us and not solely the result of genetics, the environment, unconscious influences, or luck. If we were strictly programmed by our genes or blinded by social sin and other environmental conditions, then there would be no possibility for morality. Personal morality requires making a choice. Where there is no freedom to choose, the issue of personal morality is moot.

The biological, psychological, and social sciences have certainly made us aware of how limited our freedom is. In fact, they have made us so aware that the modern day "out" for immoral and even criminal behavior is often to plead genetic, psychological, or sociological influences on conduct. Consider legal proceedings, for example. How often we hear of appeals to an array of mitigating conditions that protect the offender from bearing full responsibility for his or her actions. We hear of appeals to genetics, to social poverty, to an abusive childhood, and even to excessive television watching. One can easily conclude from all of this that we are only victims, never agents. Sometimes it seems that being victimized all but ensures being absolved from personal responsibility. Many people seem too willing to say that whatever their failing, it is not their fault—"Such and such happened to me and made me to be this way and to do these things; therefore, I can't be held responsible." I once saw a contemporary greeting card that played on this sense of being victimized and how our freedom is undermined by our past experiences. On the outside it read, "If at first you don't succeed," and on the inside it read, "Blame it on your parents." Such notions of psychological determinism have profoundly diminished our sense of responsibility and wreaked havoc on morality. Those who think of themselves as victims are the ones who look to therapy rather than to moral improvement to set their lives on track.

But just because some bad experience has happened to us in the past does not mean that it is the cause of our present misbehavior. It may be a possible influence, but not the sole cause. How is it, for example, that two people grow up in the same family with the same genetic and rearing parents, but they don't turn out the same? Not everyone responds to the same influences in the same way. So when it comes to determining influences and subsequent bad behavior, we would do well to think in degrees: How far has one been influenced? How far is one responsible? What is the next step we can take toward greater responsibility?

In the end, whatever the influences of nature or nurture, responsibility for one's actions in the present is possible. If we were absolutely determined, then we would never feel unsettled or indecisive about our choices. Neither would we ever have to deliberate about anything if we were completely free or completely determined. Nor would I be getting so many requests to speak about moral decision making, and we would certainly not need a book like this. Selling out to determinism—claiming that we are not responsible for anything—is merely an attempt to escape from freedom by claiming that we are forced to be who we are and to do what we do by the forces of heredity or environment. If we sell out, then we claim that we are not responsible for anything that we do. We might feel like the bum in the *Frank & Ernest* comic strip who is sitting on a wall conversing with his buddy. One says, "Do you believe in fate?" The other replies, "Sure, I'd hate to think I turned out like this because of something I had control over."

Sometimes, refusing to accept the freedom that is ours is a sign that we are afraid to accept responsibility for our actions. Real freedom means learning to live well within limits. Surely, all people to some degree—not only those graced with great genes, perfect parents, and an ideal social environment—are able to do the right thing. Even if we have been dealt an unpromising hand, we know that authentic living requires that we play well the hand we have been handed. Or as an old joke would have it, if someone dumps a load of lemons on your porch, don't complain. Make lemonade! Turning necessity into a virtue is one of the signs of a strong moral character. It is an expression of our capacity for self-determination.

A powerful scene from *One Flew over the Cuckoo's Nest* brings home this freedom of choice within limits quite clearly. It shows what we should be about in our moral striving as responsible adults. In this novel, McMurphy fakes insanity in order to escape a penal farm for the softer life of a mental institution. However, he comes to a head-on collision with Big Nurse, the tyrant of the ward who has psychologically emasculated her patients so that they can no longer have the freedom to choose. McMurphy begins a one-man campaign against tyranny and for freedom. In one scene he stages a showdown with Big Nurse by calling for a vote that would allow the patients to watch the World Series on TV. He is one vote short of a majority. It is up to Chief, the big Indian who, to escape the pains of tyranny, has retired into a fog where he cannot hear and cannot speak. McMurphy pleads with him to raise his hand. As Chief finds his hand going up, he begins by blaming McMurphy for it but ends up accepting his responsibility:

> It's too late to stop it now. McMurphy did something to it that first day, put some kind of hex on it....McMurphy's got hidden wires hooked to it, lifting it slow just to let me out of the fog and into the open where I'm fair game. He's doing it, wires....No, that's not the truth. I lifted it myself.[9]

This is the goal of moral striving. We need to cut short our attempted escapes from freedom so that we can responsibly claim, "I did it myself." Freedom and responsibility go hand in hand. Responsible freedom says, "I choose to do this, because I want to do it." This is quite different from the more familiar, "I really should…" or "I had better…." These all indicate that someone else is really in control. Whenever we find ourselves saying, "Actually I should…," chances are that our hearts are not in it, but we feel the external pressure of rewards if we do or of punishment if we do not. A cuckoo's nest may be an extreme image for the world in which we live, yet the neurotic is a clear image of the determined conditions we all share. The neurotic suggests that the tyranny of determining influences over which we seem to have no control has made powerlessness our chief neurosis. We all have a Big Nurse in our lives. With Chief we often retreat into the fog and attempt to escape from freedom.

However, the more we become aware of what limits us, the more we will be able to live freely within those limits. Our freedom to choose challenges us all the time. While people entangled in bad behavior that has gone on for years cannot easily turn

themselves around and do the right thing, they can do something
better than engaging in self-destructive behavior. Changing
behavior is combined with a change of attitude. Each of us has to
accept some responsibility for what he or she does. The power to
assume an attitude toward what is happening to us makes us truly
free. Dr. Viktor Frankl's testimony to human freedom and dignity, even under terrible duress in the midst of cruelty and inhu-
manity, stands out as profound witness to the limits of
conditioning factors and to the independence of mind and depth
of human freedom:

> We who lived in concentration camps can remember the
> men who walked through the huts comforting others, giv-
> ing away their last piece of bread. They may have been few
> in number, but they offer sufficient proof that everything
> can be taken away from a man but one thing: the last of the
> human freedoms—to choose one's attitude in any given set
> of circumstances, to choose one's own way.[10]

Ultimately, our freedom to choose this or that, within limits,
is fundamentally a freedom to choose an identity, to become a
certain sort of person. We cannot do everything. Determining factors prevent that. But we can pour ourselves into what we do,
make it truly our own, choose it as a genuine expression of who
we are and aspire to become.

Emotions

The film *The River's Edge* graphically illustrates that our
emotions display our moral sensitivity. It also depicts what can
happen when emotions are dulled. The story line of the film is
taken from a true incident in California when a teenage boy killed
his girlfriend for no apparent reason and then left her lying by the
river's edge. He returns to town and brags about what he has done
to his buddies. He invites them to go down to the river and look at

the dead body. They go, look, and then return home. No one does anything about it. No one calls the police, the girl's parents, or even their own parents. Nothing. Why? The movie explores the root of violence in the moral numbness of society. These teens are alienated from their emotions and from moral values. They show no empathy, no caring, no sense of sympathy. Hearing of the girl's death and then looking at her dead body does nothing to them. They look and carry on with life as usual. They are numb to emotion and to the value of life and of persons. With no feeling for what is right or wrong, no one acts in conscience.

The degree to which knowing what is right results in doing what is right depends to a great extent on the flow of emotions that support a good will. On the one hand, one can be a whiz kid at ethical theory but still be morally flawed because of the lack of affective awareness of the values at stake and a heartfelt commitment to them. Our knowledge will influence behavior to the extent that we care about the good and are committed to seeing it come about. We may be able to give a solid ethical defense for what is right (protecting another from harm out of respect for the dignity of the person) but not be able to act because we lack the emotional depth that brings life and energy to do what is required. On the other hand, some may do what is right spontaneously from the heart but not be able to give solid theoretical justification for acting that way. This shows that our moral judgments about what is the right thing to do are more than the sum of our reasons. There is an affective component as well. Our feelings display our moral sensitivity, and they drive us to act according to our convictions, even if we can't give voice to these convictions.

How many times have we found ourselves frustrated in our attempts to get others to change their behavior by simply arguing with them? We know that we are using the right information, but we see no movement toward change. Take smoking for example. By now everyone knows that smoking is bad for a person. But all the warnings on labels and in scientific papers do not convince some people to change. The power of the addiction overwhelms knowledge. But an appeal to the fear of death might have more success. Notice the way antismoking campaigns are designed. They try to scare people to change more than they try to provide new information. Clever advertisers know that to change people's behavior you must do more than give new information. You must influence their emotions. Knowing what is right will not lead to doing what is right without emotional reinforcement.

The heart is our entryway into the moral dimensions of experience. That is to say, we enter the moral enterprise of reflection, argument, and responsible living through an affective grasp of the value of persons and the web of relationships with others and the environment in which we live.[11] Feelings stimulate moral reflection and activate moral behavior. At the most general level, morality arises from an affective sense of being grasped by something that is right about a way of being human and the way things ought to be so that people can live together well in community, and it is based on an affective sense of revulsion that something is wrong about a human action and ought to be avoided. For example, the revulsion we feel when we have to look—even after many times—at a picture of prisoners of Auschwitz is a basic "ethics attack." It cries out for a remedy, a vision or standard of what ought to be. So, too, the sense of relief and satisfaction that we feel when we see someone protected from being harmed by another or rescued from a natural disaster is an "ethics attack" in the positive direction: "Yes, that's the way things ought to be." This action worthy of approval and affirmation expresses our sense of what it means to be human and to be community.

The affective dimension of morality means that conscience has affective, intuitive, imaginative, and somatic aspects as well as rational ones. So we should be suspicious of overly rationalistic accounts of conscience. The affective dimension of moral experience and an emotional commitment to value are always relevant to acting in conscience.

Not until we have the capacity for the affective experience of the value of persons and what befits their well-being will we have the capacity for acting in good conscience. All the refinements of moral reflection have developed in response to the need to bring this foundational moral experience to bear on specific cases. The ethical analyses that surround abortion, assisted suicide, capital punishment, health care reform, or the economy try to express what this foundational experience demands of us. What it demands, simply put, is that we be loving. To be moral and to be loving imply one another.

The capacity to be loving is the beginning of moral consciousness. Research on the role of empathy shows how important this human feeling is in the development of conscience.[12] When empathy is born, care is born, and with it morality. To be morally good we must be able to go out of ourselves and put ourselves in the place of another and of many others. Empathy is experiencing what another is experiencing so that the pains and pleasures of others become our own.

I once saw this portrayed vividly in a report on PBS about attempts in the Vermont state prison system to rehabilitate rapists. The goal of the rehabilitation process was to bring rapists to an experience of empathy toward their victims. The process of reform included having each rapist write out the scenario of the rape for which he was convicted. Then he had to role-play the scene with another convict. He himself took the role of his victim, with the hope that he would experience what she experienced but without the physical violation of his assault. The psychologist commented that not until the rapist could experience empathy would there be any hope of rehabilitation.

The capacity to experience an emotion like empathy belongs to our genetic endowment, but it requires the proper environment, especially in our early years, if it is ever to emerge in full power as part of the conscience of an adult. What is missing in a psychopath, for instance, is not the knowledge of right or wrong, but caring commitment to do the right thing. The psychopath has no empathy. To pour ourselves into what we do requires an emotional capacity to care about others and to commit ourselves to ideals and standards. Thus, the emotionally traumatized, the severely brain damaged, the mentally ill, and those suffering from severe pathological conditions, like the sociopath or psychopath, cannot be said to have a functioning conscience because their emotion is blunted and their self-awareness is impaired.

The effort to engage in the moral reasoning that an act of conscience demands is doomed to failure unless a person first cares enough about people and moral values to become engaged in such reflection. Without a desire to become good and do what is right, moral instruction and reflection will profit us nothing. We can give all the moral instruction we want or provide the best moral mentors we know, and create an environment where it is easy to be good, but if the person does not care about being good, nothing will happen to produce a morally good person. Emotions are the building blocks of conscience. Emotions enable us to care enough to want to commit ourselves to what we experience by heart as valuable.

The place for "reasons of the heart" is aptly demonstrated in Huckleberry Finn's inner struggle over whether he should inform Miss Watson of the whereabouts of Jim, her runaway slave, who has become his friend. Huck has been taught to obey the law. He knows in his head that he should uphold slavery and turn Jim in. Reluctantly, he writes a letter betraying Jim's whereabouts, sets it down, and then "set there thinking…and went on thinking.…" In this famous passage, Huck mulls over what he has just done against what he has experienced with Jim and in Jim. Huck's emotions and reason circle back upon each other as he lives again in his imagination what Jim has done for him and what he has done for Jim. He turns over in his heart what the two of them have learned about life and about friendship. He no longer thinks of

Jim as Miss Watson's property but as his friend. That makes all the difference.

> I see Jim before me all the time:…But somehow I couldn't seem to strike no places to harden me against him, but only the other kind…; and at last I struck the time I saved him by telling the men we had smallpox aboard, and he was so grateful, and said I was the best friend old Jim ever had in the world, and the *only* one he's got now; and then I happened to look around and see that paper [the letter he had written].
>
> It was a close place. I took it up, and held it in my hand. I was a-trembling, because I'd got to decide, forever, betwixt two things, and I knowed it. I studied a minute, sort of holding my breath, and then says to myself:
> "All right, then, I'll *go* to hell"—and tore it up.[13]

Our moral convictions, the truths we live by, do not come only by way of rational argument. They also come by way of affective experiences. Huck chose to follow his heart and save Jim from slavery. We live and reflect morally in the first place because we have an affective commitment to what we care about. Our affective commitments to the value of persons are our "reasons of the heart," which will always contribute to our moral judgments. We appeal to our "reasons of the head" to demonstrate in a way that can be rationally accessible to another what we already know by heart. Conscience is where head and heart dialogue with each other.

Conclusion

Conscience, then, is foundational to moral discernment. We all begin with this basic capacity to know good from evil. Throughout our lives we search the sources of moral wisdom to become sensitive to value, to learn virtue, and to discover what is right and what is wrong. If we are to act in conscience, we need to acquire a heartfelt awareness of what helps people to live fully and what harms them. We need to take charge and give direction to our lives lest we spend our whole lives living someone else's desires for us. We can only do this if we have sufficient emotional stability to care about ourselves and others and to commit ourselves to what we know by heart is worth striving for. Upon these foundations we can build a model of moral discernment that opens us to responding to what God is calling us to do.

CRITICAL REFLECTION:

1. How does the above presentation on conscience affirm your present understanding of conscience? *I relearned that...*
2. What new insight did you gain from this chapter? *I was surprised to learn that...*
3. What questions does this perspective raise for you? *I need to think more about...*

APPROPRIATION:

1. Share an anecdote from your life that illustrates your experience of acting in conscience. *I remember when...*
2. What would you like acting in conscience to look like for you in the future? *Next time, I want to...*

2. Practical Reasoning

PRESENT UNDERSTANDING:

- *How do you presently go about the process of deciding what you ought to do?*
- *How do you know that you are doing what God is calling you to do?*

8➤

You have just been hired by a consulting firm. It is a good position that will give financial security to your family. Your first assignment is to assess bids for a study that your client needs done. The bids were all due by 3:00 P.M. At 3:30 your boss calls you into the office. He slips one of the submitted bids into an envelope and asks you to run it over to one of the firms that you thought was going to bid on the project but had not yet done so. You are told to wait while the agent at this firm looks at the bid in the envelope and formulates his own bid to return to you. You suspect that you are being asked to cooperate in a scheme that is showing favor to your boss's friend. But as a new employee, you want to be seen as a team player. You don't want to jeopardize your job or the financial security of your family, yet it seems wrong to let a competing firm look at someone else's bid. What ought you to do?

41

"What ought I to do?" is the question that sets us on the road of practical moral reasoning. But what is the structure and dynamic of the moral reasoning process that answers this practical moral question? The task of this chapter is to give a general outline of the answer to this question.

Analogy

Making a moral decision is somewhat like walking. We do it all the time but rarely do we ever pay attention to everything that goes into it. We walk across a room every day and don't give any thought to the interplay of nerves, muscle, tendons, and bones that make walking with ease possible. Once I heard an orthopedic specialist describe what goes into taking a simple step. I was overwhelmed at the complexity. I said to myself, "If we had to be conscious of all those interrelationships before we took each step, we would probably never walk at all." Fortunately, we don't have to be conscious of what we are doing all the time. Everything works together simultaneously. Not until we begin to limp or feel like we are losing our balance do we begin to pay attention to the parts and their relationships. Have we broken a bone? Twisted a knee? Stressed one set of muscles and neglected others?

So, too, with making moral decisions. We make them all the time without ever dissecting what goes into them. But when we feel like we are losing our moral stability, then we might want to examine more closely what goes into making decisions. Where are we going wrong? Is something missing? Are we putting too much stress on one aspect to the neglect of some others?

Given the number of times that I and other moralists I know have been asked to speak on the issue of making moral decisions, there seems to be a longing in people for a method that respects the complexity of their lives. Yet there are still those who want simple answers to complex issues. For example, some common approaches that I have met to making decisions are follow the drummer and go with the flow; ask an expert for advice; do what the law requires; trust your instinct; consult the stars; "cut the scripture"; flip a coin; pray about it. These simply will not do.

I am afraid that some of our people have been seduced by thirty-second sound bites that replace well-developed arguments, or they have been lured by our "instant" culture (instant coffee, instant breakfast, instant intimacy, instant entertainment) to expect a quick-fix solution to our every need. But when it comes to living morally, we just can't "add water and stir." In moral matters, the only true road to right action is the ancient way of prudence—the skill of practical reasoning. Happily, the popular interest in ways to make a moral decision is giving us an opportunity to retrieve the skill of practical reasoning.

But what does acting prudently involve? This chapter will set us off on the road to practicing prudence by encouraging a model of practical reasoning called *moral discernment*. First, I explain that we ought to bother with moral reflection in the first place because we believe that the dignity of persons deserves it. Then I introduce in very broad strokes my model of moral discernment. The following three chapters will fill out this model by exploring the three spheres of influence that must inform the process of discernment. They are the social, situational, and personal contexts of the one who must make a moral decision.

The Need for Moral Reflection

Trying to understand what is involved in making a decision is one small part of the larger field of ethics. From the beginning, ethics has had a twofold range of interest—how to be a good person and how to make decisions that lead to right moral action. Ethics is a discipline that can make us more critical of our morality—that is, of our values, our actions, and our character—by bringing us back to thinking about what it is to be a good person. If we let our muscles of ethical reflection get flabby by failing to exercise critical thinking about what we value, about what we do, and about who we are becoming, then we can easily turn into moral cripples and lose our capacity to recognize and to avoid moral evil.

Moral values are our most basic values because they have to do with who we are as persons. Moral values are connected to the worth of persons, to the welfare of people, and to human relationships. At the level of economic values, we may say that it is unfortunate that a person is poor. At the social level, we may say that it is unfortunate that a person is computer-illiterate. But morally, if a person is a thief, a liar, an extortionist, a murderer, is unkind or unfaithful, then it is even more serious than being poor or computer-illiterate. Now we are saying something about what it means to be a person.

Consider this case. A dying friend says that he would die in peace if you promise to give two thousand dollars from his estate to someone he had cheated some years ago. You so promise. He dies. You say, "Well, he got his promise and died in peace. No one witnessed my promise, so I'm off the hook. I'll keep the money for myself."

What's wrong with this picture? Does it bother you because not following through threatens our social cohesion? Or is it that deciding to ignore the promise makes you a dishonorable person? A moral choice is not only about *doing* something; it is also about *being* a certain kind of person. We bother with moral reflection not only because we want to know what to do, but also because we want to discover the best ways to be a person and to value others as persons. Through our choices, we not only shape ourselves as persons, but we also affect the well-being of others and the moral climate in which we have to live.

Moral objectivity is grounded in those values that serve the flourishing of persons and the environment. We know that moral values are at stake when we describe actions as right or wrong, in the sense of being obligatory or prohibited. The language of rights generally indicates the presence of moral values, as does the notion of "ought" and "must." Right moral actions are those that affirm the value of persons. So when we say that something is right, we claim that persons are worth this kind of action. Or when we see on the evening news that someone has stabbed an elderly woman and stolen her car, we say that that is immoral. No one ought to do things like that. In the world of health care, we say that it is right for hospitals to make it possible for people to decide what happens to them because we believe that persons deserve this kind of control over their lives. In the world of business, we say that it is wrong for those who sell used cars to conceal the real condition of a car because we believe that persons deserve the truth in a commercial activity.

Intentionally injuring another, stealing, lying, and giving others the freedom to direct their own lives are very different kinds of actions from writing left-handed, spilling soup, or crossing the street against the light. What makes them different is that the former actions get to the heart of what it means to be human, to value persons, and to act in ways that promote the well-being of persons and community. The latter do not have such significance.

We go through a process of reflecting because we are not always clear about what best supports the value of persons. The most difficult decisions we have to make are not the ones getting the attention in the news. Everyone knows about the headliner neon moral issues, like the baboon heart transplanted into a human, the grandmother who becomes the surrogate mother for her daughter, abandoned frozen embryos that need a parent, and others. While these may be newsworthy because they present new ethical challenges brought on by technology, they are not the really hard issues that most of us have to face. The really hard choices that we are more likely to face involve issues like deciding whether or when it is time to put Mother in a nursing home. Deciding whether to submit to further medical treatment when the results are uncertain. Deciding whether to take this new job that offers high pay but leaves little time to be home. Deciding whether to go golfing again this Saturday after being away from the family for five days. Deciding whether to join a strike and force a work stoppage. Deciding whether to lend money to an alcoholic brother who is in debt, suspecting that he may just buy another drink. How do we know what love requires in these cases? What process do we use to decide?

While moral clarity is obvious in simple cases of wrongdoing, like murder, thieving, and lying, most decisions that confront us are not simple questions of right or wrong. Most of our decisions are over obligations that collide. For example, because we value persons, we say that it is right to prevent others from harm and to tell the truth. What do you do, then, when you know that your neighbor is intent on beating his wife and asks you where she is—and you know? If you give the angered husband the wrong information so as to protect his wife, you have failed to tell the truth. But if you tell the truth, you have cooperated in wife-beating. Or, on the job as an accountant with a large firm, you know that you need to stay in good graces with the company because your family relies on your steady income. But your supervisor asks you to alter an account in order to show favor to a preferred client. What do you do? To whom are you more responsible? Or what do you do with the envelope that contains the competing bid? Do you trust the boss to know what he is doing and try to be a team player? Or do you take another line of action? And what will that action be? What ought you to do?

Moral Discernment

Just as the orthopedic specialist examined the structure of the human leg to describe what happens when we walk, so I will try to get inside the heart, mind, and spirit of Christian believers making moral decisions so as to describe the pathways of moral reflection. The approach to moral reasoning described here is not a psychological model that tries to account for what is actually going on in the head of anyone who is making a decision. My aim is to describe an approach to making moral decisions that fits our fundamental commitment to God. In the Christian tradition, such an approach has been recognized as a spiritual, evaluative process. "Discernment" is the privileged name we give to the decision-making process that reaches into the heart of one's fundamental commitment to God.

As people of faith, we believe that our moral decisions are not simply a matter of solving a problem. Rather, they are a graced response to God's presence and action in our lives. As people of faith, we believe that every decision is an opportunity to respond to God, who is present in the here and now inviting us to a more abundant life. Discernment is the process of discovering the course of action most fitting to what our fundamental relationship with God demands.[1]

Unfortunately, we often associate discernment with only big decisions, like choosing a career. While it certainly includes that, discernment is also a process for living morally every day. But we don't need the same process of discernment for all decisions. Some decisions are routine, almost automatic, such as going to work and providing food and shelter for our families. We make these decisions out of habit. Still others are an obvious choice for right over wrong, such as paying for our groceries before leaving the store. These don't even require much thought. They flow naturally and routinely out of the values we live by and reflect a fundamental decision to be honest, truthful, and fair.

But then there are some decisions that are a bit more complex, such as choosing a career, supporting a social or political cause, or deciding whether to undergo more medical treatments. Decisions of this nature involve a greater investment of ourselves because they touch our hearts and affect the dominant direction of our lives. They are also decisions that are tied to complex and confusing circumstances. These are the kind that demand a fuller process of discernment because we have not developed the habit

for such decisions. The fuller process of discernment is the matter of distinguishing and discriminating between possible courses
of right actions and choosing that which best satisfies what our
relationship with God demands.

In discernment, we ask not only, "Is this action right?" but
we also ask, "Is acting this way consistent with my fundamental
commitment to God? Does it fit who I am and who I want to
become as a disciple of Jesus for today?" Making moral decisions from the point of view of faith looks for the right thing to do
in light of our most fundamental relationship in life—our commitment to God. As a people of faith, we want to know what God
is requiring of us, not just what the law or conventional behavior
requires. The work of conscience is to discover the call of God in
each situation in order to know what God is asking of us in the
here and now. Moral discernment, then, is something more than
disciplined deliberation. It is a graced exercise of faith seeking to
express itself in action.

To put it briefly and most generally, what God is asking of us
is to be alive with love. Living morally is about loving. The Christian moral life is fundamentally about love flowing from our experience of God's self-giving love in Jesus. To follow the way of
Jesus as disciples are bound to do is to be informed and animated
by loving God, neighbor, and self. In the synoptic gospels, Jesus
summarizes moral living with the words, "Love God and love
your neighbor as you love yourself" (Mk 12:28–32; Mt 22:37–40;
Lk 10:25–28). In John's gospel, Jesus says "Love one another as I
have loved you" (15:12).

The Christian community professes that morality is
grounded in God's self-giving love in Jesus. Our response of faith
to God's self-giving love must show itself in love. While being loving remains our overall moral concern, what love demands must be
specified in each area of life. But how do we know what love
demands? Love needs a model and a method. Without them, love is
lost. When we try to declare what love demands in a particular

situation, we draw upon many different resources and use different approaches. No wonder we often meet many different positions on what to do. The strategy for love that I want to present here is the art of discerning what God is asking of us. We need to develop this art if we are going to love well as disciples of Jesus living amid conflicting claims of value.

But to develop this art and to engage in the process of discernment requires a degree of faith and personality development that enables us to have a sufficient grasp of how God acts in our lives and of who we are. If we do not have faith so as to be open to the presence of God or if we lack sufficient self-possession so as to give direction to our lives or are not sufficiently emotionally stable so that we can care about others and commit ourselves to standards and ideals, then we are not ready for discernment as a disciplined art of moral reflection. Moreover, if we have been living our lives by only doing what we are told to do because someone in authority with power over us has told us to do it or because of peer pressure, then we are not yet mature enough for moral discernment.

The following description of moral discernment presupposes sufficient personal faith, and moral development at the same time points the way to mature moral reflection by identifying what goes on in the process of discovering the particular way to be loving that God is requiring of us now.

A Model of Moral Discernment

One of the great failures in moral discernment is moral myopia. That is, we don't see enough of what is involved. Some people fix on authority to tell them what to do; others rely just on intuition; still others will follow the crowd. While each of these sources offers something, no one by itself is enough. Each bears only limited moral information. What I want to sketch here is a model of what goes into a holistic process of moral discernment.

The analogy that I most frequently find people using in reference to moral decision making is the analogy of solving a problem. That so many would draw such an analogy is not surprising. Our scientifically oriented world thrives on seeing something as a problem and trying to solve it. So we are well disposed to make every area of our lives an extension of the experimental method of reasoning so well accepted in our scientific world. This method gives us a clarity of procedure and certainty of conclusion that we have come to expect in other areas of life as well. Clarity and certainty in moral matters have a strong appeal, especially as we face explosive changes in church, society, and culture; increasing moral complexity in our lives; and growing moral diversity in our communities. But practical moral reasoning requires a certain amount of insight and experienced perception that cannot be mediated by the linear reasoning we are accustomed to use when facing a problem. The qualitative assessments that must go into practical reasoning require a discerning sensibility.

The practical reasoning of moral discernment is an art form. That is, it is more than a linear sequence of stepwise logical procedures. Discernment discovers what is the reasonable thing to do by engaging not only the head but also the heart. In and around the linear flow of discursive reasoning, discernment is an experienced perception involving the back-and-forth, around-and-about movement of intuition, affective sensibility to values, and subtle assessments of the relationships of multiple factors. When we embark down the road of the practical moral reasoning of discernment, we commit ourselves to a process that, like a four-stranded cable, circles back upon itself to intertwine *faith, reason, emotion,* and *intuition.*[2] *Faith* gives us a perspective and framework for interpreting what is going on and for setting priorities. *Reason* helps us assess further the scope of our moral experience and study the multiple relationships of the factors that make it up. *Emotion* and *intuition* give us our first evaluation of what is going on and an idea of the obligations and responsibilities we have toward the situation.

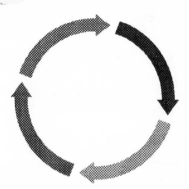

When we say that we are "wrestling with a problem," "mulling it over," or "praying about it," what we mean is that we are seeking the harmony of these four strands by engaging the back-and-forth, around-and-about movement of head and heart. The harmony of these strands is confirmed by the experience of

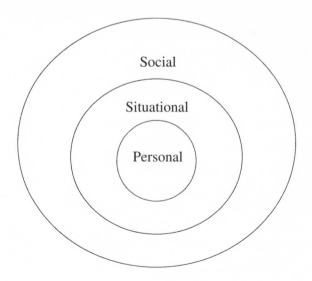

interior balance and peace that gives us the confidence that this is what God is calling us to do. Moral wisdom ultimately rests on such a discerning sensibility, not on the crisp conclusions of a linear process of discursive reasoning.

In the process of coming to harmony of faith, reason, emotion, and intuition, we need to appeal to the three realms of inquiry, or three spheres of influence, that inform moral reflection. The most general is the *social context,* which contains the many sources of wisdom and experience that influence our perception and inform our evaluation. Closer to the conscience is the *situational context,* which explores the relevant circumstances that make a situation unique. Finally, there is the immediate *personal context* of ourselves as moral agents who are experiencing the moral complexity of the situation, trying to understand the moral demands of love, and then deciding what action best promotes the value of persons in response to the call of God in the moment. While each of these contexts must be included for full moral discernment, not all elements from each are morally relevant to the same degree in every case.

Without claiming to be exhaustive, the next three chapters will examine some of the outstanding points of reference in each context to see what they contribute to the art of moral discernment.

CRITICAL REFLECTION:

1. How does the above presentation on practical reasoning affirm your present approach to making decisions? *I relearned that…*
2. What new insight did you gain from this chapter? *I was surprised to learn that…*
3. What questions does your new learning raise for you? *I need to think more about…*

APPROPRIATION:

1. Share an anecdote from your life that illustrates how you can go about making up your mind. *I remember when...*
2. What would you like your method of making a decision to look like now? *Next time, I want to...*

II. Moral Discernment

3. Social Context

PRESENT UNDERSTANDING:

- *What resources from your present social context do you use most often in making a moral decision?*
- *Of all the communities or worlds in which you participate, which has the greatest influence on your moral perspective?*

☙

Remember how surprised we felt the first time that we saw the breathtaking view of our blue planet seen from the surface of the moon? We had never seen our planet that way before because we had never stood on the moon to look back. Where we stand defines what we see. For this reason, I begin with our social context. What we see, how we think, and what we choose are shaped largely by where we stand, that is, our social location. We cannot be completely autonomous in making a moral choice because the social realities that surround us strongly influence our sense of value and virtue. We acquire a sense of moral values and virtues much the same way that we learn a native language; namely, by living with people who behave in a certain way. Thus, our interpersonal relations are the major influence on forming our values and our virtues and on setting limits within which our freedom operates. We come to know what sort of person we ought to be

57

and what we ought to do by being in the company of others, especially those who are committed to seeking the good and striving to embody it.[1]

As we grow up, we internalize the beliefs and values of the communities that have the greatest influence on us. As a result, our moral education is less a matter of memorizing rules of behavior and more a matter of appropriating a particular way of living, of acquiring a set of images for interpreting life, and of fashioning patterns of acting to make life worth living according to what is approved or disapproved by our most formative communities. This chapter will give a brief sketch of various social sources of moral information and influence, religious and nonreligious, that inform the process of discernment.

I will begin with sources of moral influence from our religious world. I begin here not because the religious world is chronologically the first to influence us or even because it is necessarily the most influential. I begin with it because we believe that it provides us with the truthful way of interpreting the way the world ought to be, of what our sense of values and virtues ought to be, and of showing us who we ought to be and become. For brevity's sake, I will discuss only three principle sources of moral influence that our religious world provides—the Bible, Jesus, and the church.

Religious Sources

Bible

The Bible has served generations as a source of inspiration through its stories of heroic people and their deeds (Abraham and Sarah, Moses and Miriam, David, Jeremiah, Deborah, Ruth, Jesus, Mary, Paul). It is both a source of *revealed morality,* through its commandments, parables, and the radical sayings of Jesus, and also a source of *revealed reality,* through its images and themes.[2] When we use the Bible today, we are much more conscious of its historically conditioned character. So we apply biblical themes, images, and commands carefully to our present circumstances.[3]

Certainly the commandments have long been used as a primary source of revealed morality. But we need to ask what is really being commanded by "Honor your father and mother," for example. When we look at the context of the commandment, we learn that it is not a commandment addressed to children emphasizing implicit obedience. Instead, it is a commandment addressed to the entirety of Israel, urging that all honor their parents, that is, acknowledge them as persons of importance and worth. The temptation was strong in ancient Israel, as it would be for any nomadic people, to banish those who were no longer useful—the aged, the weak, the sick. The commandment counters such action. Responsibility to fulfill the commandment lies not so much upon children as upon adults to provide service necessary to support their aged parents. The commandment is a clear affirmation that human value is based on something other than one's functional abilities.[4] To use the Bible properly as revealed morality, then, we have to do the critical work of understanding what the prescriptions for behavior really mean in context.

In the gospels, how are we to understand the radical sayings of Jesus, such as "Give to everyone who asks; go the extra mile; turn the other cheek" (Mt 5:38–42)? Are these commands to be obeyed literally, or instead, are they counsels of imaginative inspiration to stretch our way of seeing things and to make us aware of the distance between our motivations and the novel revolution of the reign of God calling us to conversion?

Another way of using the Bible is as revealed reality. The Bible's great images highlight the contours and patterns of our lives and influence the way we interpret our experience. Consulting the Bible for the light it sheds on human experience is called the illuminative use of scripture.[5] Using this method, we make decisions in the light of biblical themes and we derive our basic orientation in life and our framework of meaning from them. For example, the "covenant" has been one of the master images of contemporary ethics. It conveys the sense that we are people who live interdependently in solidarity with one another. It says that our relationships ought to be based on freedom, motivated by love, respectful of the dignity of persons, and held together by trust. It makes love and fidelity our primary virtues.

"Creation" is another influential biblical motif. It illumines our special dignity of being made in the image of God. It helps us see that we are creatures who live connected to all created reality and in ultimate dependence on God as the source of life. Our concern with ecology draws a great deal from this biblical image.

In the New Testament, the "reign of God" and "community" are two strong images for interpreting the goal of human efforts to bring all people into right relationships of justice and peace. "Death-resurrection" has also been used to great effect to provide a context of meaning for interpreting suffering. So the Bible remains a rich resource for inspiration, direction, and illumination of moral living, even if it is not a thesaurus of answers.

Jesus

For Christians, the words and deeds of Jesus are the starting point of ethics. We believe that Jesus is the ultimate norm of the moral life, the paradigmatic figure to whom we turn to discover what it means to be a person and to live a life fully responsive to God.[6] It follows that not to think from the perspective of the story of Jesus is a moral failure of great significance. To accept Jesus as the norm of the moral life is to respond to his summons to discipleship. This summons asks us, "What sort of person am I to become as a follower of Jesus?" and "What sort of life am I to live as one who recognizes Jesus as the authoritative expression of what it means to live in full response to God?"

Imitation of Christ

We commonly speak of this call to discipleship as living the imitation of Christ. But we must not confuse imitation with mimicry. Mimicry replicates external behavior. It asks, "What would Jesus do?" Although this question is well intentioned, it is not the question that guides authentic imitation. It only opens us to another form of fundamentalism that wants to copy Jesus point for point. It fails to respect the historically conditioned nature both of Jesus as a first-century Palestinian Jew and of the biblical texts that reveal him to us. Just as we would not want to say that accepting Jesus as norm requires that we be carpenters, Jewish, male, and itinerant preachers, so we do not want to say that we must die at the hands of political and religious leaders because Jesus did, and so forth. Such mimicry is the death of any creative response to the different demands of our own day.

not mimicry

What does imitation demand? Perhaps a story can help. A young artist wanted to paint landscapes that were as great as her teacher's. But try as she might, she could never succeed. "Perhaps," she thought, "if I use my teacher's brushes, then I will produce great art." But even with them, she could not achieve her goal. The teacher, on seeing her frustrated efforts, said, "It is not my brushes that you need, but my spirit."

Authentic imitation is living in the spirit of Jesus. We are to acquire the dispositions and values of Jesus so that we can be creatively responsive to the needs of our day in ways that harmonize with the way of life exemplified in Jesus. So rather than asking, "What would Jesus do?" we ought to ask, "How can we be as faithful in our obedience to God and in giving loving service to others in our day as Jesus was in his?" This question calls on us to do more than comb the pages of the New Testament for particular teachings of Jesus. Rather, it calls us to let our imaginations be stirred by the story of Jesus that we find in the gospels. In this way, we can come to see how our character and actions might harmonize with his by way of analogy in the situations of our day.[7]

When we look to the gospels to see what kind of life Jesus lived, we can see how we ought to act—with self-sacrificial love—even if we can't tell precisely what we are to do. The stories of Jesus help to evoke dispositions that motivate us to center ourselves on God and to take seriously what he took seriously. What he took seriously was the reign of God. People most in need of justice and reconciliation were close to his heart. What Jesus did and for whom he did things should help us see human needs differently and provide us a disposition and orientation for meeting them.

The stories of Jesus also tell us who we are to become, as individuals and as a community. Jesus lived in a way that set people free. We must ask whether our relationships imitate his in the ways we influence others to become who they are and to use their gifts for the sake of the community.

Church

The church provides moral guidance through the way it preserves the scriptures and the apostolic faith in Jesus so that each person may be able to find Christ and walk with him through life. The church does this in many ways. The ways it uses its resources of people, institutions, money, and liturgical life are some. But most often we think of the church serving as a moral teacher when it promulgates official statements on current moral issues.[8] So often we want to know, "What does the church say about…?" While the church hasn't said something about everything, it has said something about a lot of moral issues of our day. In this way, the church is helping us see how we can keep the vision of the gospel alive when facing new problems through the ages. We need the guidance of the church today and in every age because our own sinfulness and the sinfulness of social structures can too easily prevent us from seeing the demands of the gospel for today. Moreover, there are many moral matters (such as bioethics and economic matters) that require a specialized knowledge that many of us have neither the time nor resources to acquire. So we can be grateful that the church as teacher draws upon specialists to compose its statements and to clarify issues so that we can learn how to relate to them in faith.

Vatican II taught us the proper relationship of conscience to magisterial teaching in moral matters in the way it affirmed the primacy of conscience. A particularly significant position is found in the *Declaration on Religious Freedom,* n. 14. This text has since been repeated by Pope John Paul II in his encyclical *Veritatis Splendor* (n. 64) to show the proper use of magisterial teaching in the formation of conscience. The text reads, "In forming their consciences the Christian faithful must give careful attention to the sacred and certain teaching of the church." An earlier rendering of this text at the Second Vatican Council read "ought to form their consciences according to the teaching of the church." The rendering "according to" was rejected for being overly restrictive.

By accepting the less restrictive reading "must give attention to," the council and then the encyclical both affirm that the moral teaching of the magisterium, under the guidance of the Holy Spirit, carries a weight and presumption of truth for Catholics that no other teacher can rightfully claim. Official teaching is an extremely significant resource that must be given a preference over other considerations in the responsible formation of conscience. We must assume that official teaching expresses an aspect of moral truth and must try, under the guidance of the Holy Spirit, to appropriate the truth it enshrines. Therefore, Catholics must give due deference to official teaching and include it in making a moral decision. As Pope John Paul II goes on to say, after repeating the instruction of the council on the relation of conscience to the magisterium,

> It follows that the authority of the Church, when she pronounces on moral questions, in no way undermines the

> freedom of conscience of Christians....The Church puts
> herself always and only at the *service of conscience,* help-
> ing it to avoid being tossed to and fro by every wind of doc-
> trine proposed by human deceit....(*VS,* n. 64)

When we turn to an official teaching of the church for moral
guidance, then, we do so because we want to learn from it. In
humility, we recognize our own limits of experience and knowledge that prevent us from grasping the whole of moral truth about
an issue. We trust the church as a reliable guide of moral wisdom,
and so we want to stretch our experience and vision of making
the gospel come alive. We listen to the teaching of the church, try
to discern its truth, and incorporate it into the entire process of
informing conscience and making a decision. While we insist
that a loyal Catholic must include the teaching of the church in
the process of discernment, we do not mean to eliminate all the
other sources of moral knowledge and experience that good discernment requires—thus, the need for prudence informed by a
fuller process of moral discernment.

Nonreligious Sources

In addition to living in a religious world, we live in many
other worlds that are not specifically religious but still very formative of our sense of moral value and virtue. To some of these I
now turn.

Communities of Influence

Our special relationships of family, friends, ethnic community, neighborhood, and school, for example, already have patterns of practice and expectations that inform most of our actions.
In these communities of influence, we learn what it is that we are
to value about persons. We identify instinctively with the ways of

thinking and acting that we see supported by the community. We learn what constitutes moral outrage or moral favor by listening to conversations or by seeing what our families approve or don't. The ways we experience people treating each other in these communities are also moral lessons for us. In one group, for example, we learn that women do not count, or black people must be kept invisible. In another, we see that food is always shared with the neighbors, children are celebrated, and the old and weak are always cared for within the family. We internalize moral imperatives when we watch and listen to what a group admires and to what it finds unacceptable.

In the U.S., for example, many people highly value personal autonomy. They don't want anyone interfering with the way they pursue their personal plans. But the individualism that such a view of autonomy produces is not as highly prized in Hispanic or Asian cultures, where filial piety and family identity tend to prevail. I have learned from the students of non-European background in my medical ethics classes, for example, that Vietnamese, Koreans, and Mexican-Americans are less likely to want to be told the diagnosis and prognosis of a serious illness. They don't want to know because the family makes the decisions anyway. They believe that the family will know what to do when the right time comes. Whereas it has become common to use a skilled nursing facility to care for the frail elderly, the members of an Asian culture would probably find such institutionalization of the elderly to be an offense to human dignity. So we should not be surprised if their decision about what to do with Grandma differs from ours. These few examples show that ingrained cultural attitudes and practices already determine, to a great extent, what choices we have available to us.

Communities of influence keep values alive. Each community has built-in moral messages about what is expected of a good member. It keeps these expectations alive through its literature, art, and social practices. In our culture, moral messages—like

"Live and let live," "Me first," "Look out for #1," or "I owe it to myself"—are powerfully conveyed through television, movies, magazines, music, and newspapers. So it is important that we pay attention to the schools our children attend, the friends they keep, the books they read, the television programs they watch. We can't escape the influence of the communities that surround us. So when we begin to do moral reflection, we don't come at our issue like fresh film in a camera. We are already filled with images of the way persons are to be treated. These images influence what we see and what we value. When we realize that living morally is not in the first instance about resolving conflicting values but about descriptive and interpretive skills of our character, then we will pay greater attention to the communities that provide us images for shaping our vision and our values.

To examine your vision and values, consider yourself in the center of a series of concentric circles. Each circle represents one of the communities in which you live, such as family, church, school, friends, ethnic community, political party, entertainment world, the world of sports, professional associations, and the like. Different communities may be placed closer to the center for different issues because they have a greater influence on your perception and value

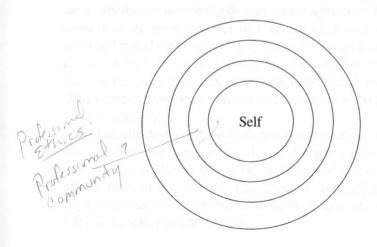

of what is important to you. How would you line up the communi- *Over* ties from those having the greatest to the least influence on your approach to the morality of using drugs, homosexuality, divorce, single-parent families, care of the dying, or whatever moral issue you have to face?

I want to single out one community that is underrated for its place in the development of a moral person and thus for its influence on how and what we choose. That is the special community of friends.[9] We have all heard it said, "You are known by the friends you keep." There is truth to this statement, because friendship is the school of forming character. If we want to become good and do what is right, we need the support of others who share our vision and values and who are committed to seeing them fulfilled in us. That is what friends do for one another. Friendship is the context in which we come together to encourage and support one another in a shared vision of what is important in life and how to achieve it.

From the perspective of Christian morality, we need people who share our conviction that discipleship matters. As an influence on moral choice, friends teach us how to be devoted to one another for their own sake, how to care for them, and how to identify with them and the values they uphold. If we did not have the support of others who shared our values, our personal values would have little hope of surviving. Left on our own without friends, we would have a hard time becoming virtuous. Without friends, we can quickly grow disenchanted with our vision of what is important in life, doubt our values, and question their importance. But by sharing life with others who are also striving to become good, we learn what goodness is and how to achieve it.

Living in a pluralistic world of diverse communities of influence is a good news/bad news story. The good news is that, by participating in different communities, we can compare and contrast experiences to broaden our moral awareness and to relativize our moral perspectives. The bad news is that, when our communities of influence get too diverse, we can lose a sense of shared values and weaken our support for whatever values we hold. Consider the purpose of the process envisioned in the Rite of Christian Initiation of Adults (RCIA). We want candidates to participate in the life of the Catholic community as much as possible so that they will be able to experience and identify with values of the Catholic tradition. If they are only loosely affiliated with us, they would never acquire a Catholic identity, vision, or way of life. The conversion process and rites of initiation are conducted with the conviction that becoming Catholic requires spending time with people who already are Catholic and are striving to be so even more.

In the end, we cannot hide from the various communities of influence on us. Moral thought is largely a social product. Not until we become critically aware of the influence of these communities will we be able to be freed of their determining influence so that we can choose, not on the basis of external pressure, but out of responsible freedom.

Role Models

In making decisions, wisdom directs us to any source that will throw light on an issue and help make the elements in the decision more visible. Most of our moral decisions probably do not come as the result of some abstract reasoning process anyway. They are more likely due to the influence of someone we admire for wisdom, experience, or knowledge. We learn how to act by paying attention to the decision-making process and to the moral actions of others—thus, the importance of role models and experts.

In one of the *Peanuts* cartoons, Linus quotes Oscar Wilde, saying, "Nothing worth knowing can be taught." In other words, most of the valuable lessons in life are caught by experience more than they are passed on by argument. The experiences we have of influential people who have caught our imaginations are all-important for what and how we decide.

Our moral mentors can come out of literature and history as

well as from our immediate experience in life. The popularity of William Bennett's *Book of Virtues*[10] can be seen as a longing for moral models of virtuous behavior. From literature, for example, we can witness the jealousy and pride that pull down Othello and King Lear and marvel as Macbeth gains a kingdom but loses his soul. We can be inspired to do good despite the cost by watching Thomas More or Jane Eyre let integrity triumph over adversity. Of course, reading about the character and fate of Othello, Lear, Macbeth, Thomas More, Jane Eyre, and others does not in itself instill virtue, but it can stir our feelings to make us care about what happens to anyone who would try to live like them. This emotional arousal is the beginning of thinking about morality and developing character. It is possible that we can discover parts of ourselves to reform or to develop by meeting great characters of literature such as these.

Within our communities of influence are certain people who make a moral way of living so attractive that we want to imitate them. A sponsor in the RCIA process can be such a person. Role models present us with living images of what it means to hold a certain role (father, mother, teacher, banker). So we can look to them to know what would be an appropriate style and function for someone in that role. For example, good fathers play with their children, read to them, and listen to their stories. While we ought not to imitate a role model in a slavish way, since each situation differs, we can catch something of the spirit, style, and disposition for the way we face conflict and live according to our values. Who has so fascinated you that you would like to fashion your life in a similar way? People who fascinate us probably influence our moral choices more than abstract principles do.

Expert Authority

Consulting with an expert for individual decisions in an ever-growing, complex world is a very wise way of proceeding

before making a decision. The expert can help us see dimensions
of an experience we would otherwise miss. For example, when
investing money, we want to be sure we talk to someone who
understands investments and their implications before we risk
our hard-earned money. Likewise, no one would want to make a
decision about a serious medical intervention without thorough
consultation with a medical specialist. For good discernment we
need to test our judgments against the advice and perception of
others whose experience and perspective we respect.

Laws

Laws and principles are probably what most people turn to
first in trying to make a decision. In many instances, these will be
the most significant resource we have. "Keep the law and the law
will keep you" is a motto that has guided the life of many. Without laws and principles, we would be dangerously tossed about
on the rough seas of moral chaos. The familiar cry, "There ought
to be a law!" or the call for clear principles has strong appeal in
the face of moral diversity and complexity. There will always be
a temptation to impose a law or principle in a desperate quest for
stability and certainty. But while at once affirming the value of
laws and principles in the moral life, we need to be aware, at the
same time, of their proper function in guiding us through the
process of discernment and of their limitations as a resource for
making a decision.

Because the order of law and the order of morality are so
closely related, they are frequently confused. Since laws legislate
morality in the public order, we readily think that what is legal is
moral. If something is not against the law, so we think, then it
must be morally acceptable. This relation of law and morality is
generally true. For the most part we can rely on the law as a moral
guide in making decisions. But not always. Moral obligations can
and often do exceed what the law requires, such as in paying a

just wage or in securing informed consent for a medical treatment. Moral obligation requires disobedience to an unjust law. The mentality that equates what is morally required with what the law demands too easily gives way to minimalism and a spiritual laziness that only stifles initiative and conversion. Such a mentality relies too heavily on the law to define the scope of moral responsibility. What we need, rather, is to exercise moral muscle and engage in moral discernment.

Laws can be helpful as moral guides because laws identify certain values and challenge us to promote them. As expressions of value, laws can help us find our way through moral confusion. But sometimes the law is not the best safeguard of public order or of moral value, as we experienced with our laws that supported racial discrimination. In such cases, moral responsibility supersedes the law. While we want to approach the laws with the presumption in their favor, we must also recognize the limitations of law. We must be ready to criticize the law for its shortcomings and have the courage to refuse to cooperate with the law when it does not serve justice. The Catholic tradition of resisting unjust laws accounts for as much. All laws are relative to what love requires. Sometimes the law does not yet recognize what love demands.

Principles

Some moral principles, such as the ten commandments, have come to us from revelation; other principles have come to us from accumulated human wisdom, such as "be true to yourself," "one favor deserves another," or "to each according to his or her due." Principles are like laws in that they, too, represent the moral memory of the community. Unlike laws, however, principles do not carry with them any public sanction if we do not follow them.

Principles are necessary in moral discernment. For one thing, they help us interpret important aspects of our moral situation, such as "protect the innocent from harm." They also point the way toward fulfilling our duties, such as "keep secrets," "tell the truth," and "give help to those in need." Because we have principles, we don't have to reinvent the wheel every time we need to make a decision. Principles save us from moral paralysis. They take the pressure off the really hard decisions because they reflect prudential insight and bear the wisdom of collective experience that we can rely on to direct us toward what befits human well-being. They point to values we must take into account, such as life, truth, and privacy. Sometimes they tell us how to act toward these values, such as "do not take the life of an innocent person," "do not lie," "do not gossip." So it would be a mistake to underestimate the contribution that principles can make to our discernment. While they may not be able to tell us everything, there is still a lot that we can learn from the wisdom enshrined in them. By turning to principles, then, we can broaden our moral outlook, become sensitive to moral dimensions of experience, and grow in prudence.[11]

Some principles are absolute. In the Roman Catholic moral tradition, they are commonly expressed in terms of intrinsic evils. In *Veritatis Splendor,* Pope John Paul II repeats the list from the Second Vatican Council's document *Gaudium et Spes* (n. 27) to illustrate those actions that are never to be done:

> Whatever is hostile to life itself, such as any kind of homicide, genocide, abortion, euthanasia and voluntary suicide; whatever violates the integrity of the human person, such as mutilation, physical and mental torture and attempts to coerce the spirit; whatever is offensive to human dignity, such as subhuman living conditions, arbitrary imprisonment, deportation, slavery, prostitution and trafficking in women and children; degrading conditions of work which treat laborers as mere instruments of profit, and not as free responsible persons....(*VS,* n. 80)

Principles forbidding acts such as these are to be taken as absolutes because they have a value judgment built into their very meaning. These bind everyone in the same way and to the same degree. Since they do not allow for any legitimate exception, they do not leave room for acting in any other morally acceptable way. Once we can say that a moral absolute prohibits a certain kind of action (murder, torture, stealing, prostitution, rape), then the only morally good act is to obey the absolute principle and refrain from the forbidden action (cf. *VS,* n. 67).

But there are other principles that are generally applicable but not always so. These apply in most cases, but there may be instances when they conflict with another pressing obligation. For example, the principle of confidentiality binds unless it conflicts with the demands of justice to protect an innocent party from harm. Or take promise keeping. Generally we ought to keep a promise. If you promise your children to take them to the movies and, on the way, come upon an accident where your immediate assistance is needed, then the duty to care for those in need would override the duty to keep the promise. In each case, the burden of proof to act contrary to the principle falls on the one who would go against it. The proper use of limited principles, such as confidentiality and promise keeping, requires an openness to the Spirit as a source of empowerment to distinguish subtle differences among otherwise similar circumstances. This is precisely the work of the well-ordered heart in the art of discernment.

Another limitation of this kind of principle is that, while it may tell us what is important about being human (to be free, to be safe, to be respected), it does not tell us what is more important in a given case. No problems would exist if making a decision could be reduced to applying principles and if there were only one relevant principle for each case. But in most cases there is more than one principle making its claim on us. For example, if we tell the truth, we may not be saving someone from being harmed; or if we save someone from harm, then we do not tell the truth. We have to ask which principle (protect the vulnerable from harm or tell the truth) connects with the case at hand and better serves the human values at stake.

The attraction of principles in making decisions has been to save us from the errors of situationalism and to counter the pull to subjectivism and to relying on emotions alone to lead us. But as important as principles are, they are not the center of moral discernment. Principles need to be interpreted, as do the situations to which they must be applied. But we do not ever want to ignore principles. They help us by giving us a vision of the important dimension of values in experience. Absolute negative prohibitions even tell us clearly what to avoid. But most of our moral decisions for everyday living are not governed by such absolutes, such as whether or when to put Mother in the nursing home, whether to submit to further medical treatment, or whether to take a job that requires being away from home five days a week. Most of our decision making requires a discerning sensibility that thinks along with the wisdom enshrined in generally applicable principles and that takes into consideration a full account of the situation in which the decision has to be made and the personal context of the one making the decision. To these we turn next.

Conclusion

These, then, are some of the major sources of moral information and influence from our social worlds that play a significant role in the process of discernment. They shape our sense of value and virtue, affect the way we interpret what is going on, and so ultimately influence what we will judge to be the right thing to do. But the social context alone is not enough for discernment. We must also make a careful reading of the situation in which we have to act. We turn next, then, to the situational context.

CRITICAL REFLECTION:

1. How does the above presentation on the social context of moral discernment affirm your present use of social resources? *I relearned that...*
2. What new insight did you gain from this chapter? *I was surprised to learn that...*
3. What questions does your new learning raise for you? *I need to think more about...*

APPROPRIATION:

1. Share an anecdote from your life that illustrates how you have been influenced by social resources and have turned to them to shape your decisions. *I remember when...*
2. How would you like to include social resources in your process of making a decision? *Next time, I want to...*

4. Situational Context

PRESENT UNDERSTANDING:

- *What aspects of the situation surrounding your moral problems have the greatest influence on determining what you ought to do?*
- *What questions do you ask yourself in order to uncover the moral dimensions of your situation?*

⅌➤

What God is asking of me in the here and now cannot be known without a critical understanding of the situation itself. How I ought to express my relationship to God in this instance can only become clear once I understand the circumstances that make up my situation.

The situational context is where we meet moral values. While no two situations may be exactly alike, they may be similar enough to warrant bringing to bear on them the accumulated wisdom enshrined in a moral principle. Situations, however, may also have enough dissimilarity to warrant close scrutiny to identify important new features that may require a different kind of response.

If we were to live by principles alone, we would be living by generalizations. For example, "it is wrong to kill" is a generalization that we can rely on. It gets us through most situations where life is at stake. But moral discernment requires that we do the hard work of making distinctions when there are real differences. For example, what if your life is being threatened by a crazed gunman? With this new feature of the situation, the principle "do not kill" may not be the best strategy for protecting the value of human life. In this situation, killing may be morally right. So we must pay attention to the total moral reality so that we can include all morally relevant features that make each case different.

At this point in explaining this model of discernment, I am often challenged by the objection, "You are only promoting a disguised form of situation ethics." Not so. Paying attention to the details of the situation does not mean that we are endorsing situation ethics. Situation ethics wants to make love the only law by doing away with any other principles as absolutely binding. It says that there are no other overarching values or any objective moral order from which we can declare some actions as always wrong regardless of the circumstances. However, we know that situations are similar enough to be guided by some common values and principles even if they are dissimilar according to morally significant differences. So without abandoning principles and a sense of an objective moral order, we ought to take the situational context seriously. We do so by asking enough questions about the situation in order to uncover its morally relevant features and to determine which of them are significant enough to determine the morally right thing to do.

People often disagree about what to do because they work with different readings of the moral reality. If we do not do a thorough investigation of the situation, we may miss some clues that point us in the direction of what is the right thing to do. Even after we investigate as thoroughly as we can, the moral solution of what we ought to do may still not be perfectly clear. One of the hazards in ethics is an uncontrolled passion to get everything squared away. But we must remember that in living the moral life, we can't escape the burden of having to decide while there is still ambiguity. Too many people demand certitude from moral reflection when all we can produce are modest conclusions. We must learn to live in a world of shades of gray more than in a world of black and white.

This chapter will show how to make a reasonably thorough investigation of the situation by asking questions that uncover the moral dimensions of the situation where we will find the moral values we must choose.[1] These questions are not always of equal moral importance, nor will answers to them provide infallible moral direction. But they do help us uncover the moral dimensions of the situation and draw closer to what God is asking of us.

What?

The first question is obvious, but not always easy to answer. What is going on? This question fixes our attention on getting the facts straight. It is the first step in any rational decision-making process. We have to know what is going on before we can discover what we are to do. What we think is going on affects our attitudes and behavior toward the situation under consideration.

How we answer "what?" directs our search for what we ought to do in relation to it. In short, our answer sets us up for all the other questions we have to ask. If we answer the "what?" with an evaluation, such as "this is an abortion" or "this is stealing," then we do not have to go any further. We have already made a judgment about the morality of the action in question. If, however, we are not yet able to make a moral evaluation of the action and can only answer the question in descriptive, morally neutral language, such as "ending a life" or "taking someone's property," then we must go on to ask the remaining questions in order to unlock the moral implications of the situation at hand. A good example of the difference between a description and an evaluation is in the way we talk about taking life. We commonly distinguish between a murder and a homicide. Homicide is descriptive.

It gives us a perspective without judging. We know there can be justifiable homicides, but never a justifiable murder. Murder is an evaluative term. It always means "wrongful killing." Ultimately, murder may be the final judgment. But it would be premature to name the action of taking life as murder before we have examined the full context of the killing. So how we name what is going on makes a difference in how we respond to it.

Why? and How?

Next come "why?" and "how?" These questions focus on the ends and the means. A popular error is to think that if our goal is good, then the means must automatically be good since it brings us to our intended end. This is the typical "ends justify the means" argument. But we also know that the road to hell is paved with good intentions. Intention is not all that matters. The "why?" cannot be separated from the other questions that must be asked if we are to disclose the full moral reality. Well-intentioned people do harmful things to achieve their end. For example, what seems to be a gift at the "what?" level can be a political bribe at the "why?" level. For example, in health care we believe that every doctor intends what is best for patients, but that doesn't mean that "doctor knows best" in every case so that whatever the doctor wants is all right to do. What seems like withdrawing life-support systems so as to allow the disease to run its natural course can be an act of killing or murder when we know the "why?" In family life, how we go about correcting a child in order to achieve socially acceptable behavior can properly shape a child's behavior or it can be physically hurtful and harm the child's sense of worth. It all depends on how we discipline. To provide for the family and to fulfill ourselves, we get a job. But if our job becomes so all-consuming that we have no time for the family, then we have made our means become our end to the detriment of family and self. So how we go about achieving our end ought to matter to us more than the fact of getting it. To sharpen the focus, we cannot do whatever we want in order to achieve our end. We have to see how all the features uncovered by the reality-revealing questions relate to one another, not just how the ends relate to the means.

The "how?" question also discloses some acts that are always unacceptable as a means. These are prohibited by absolute principles, as we saw in the last chapter, and are such actions as those identified in *Veritatis Splendor,* n. 80, as "hows" that must always be avoided. But in addition to helping us uncover actions that we must always avoid, these questions also help us pay attention to moral character. How and why we act shape and reveal the kind of person we are and are becoming. Cheating produces cheaters, gossiping produces gossips, whereas keeping a secret produces a trustworthy person, and following through on a commitment produces a faithful person. How and why we act can weaken or strengthen our moral character. This is the wisdom enshrined in the aphorism, "It doesn't matter whether you win or lose, it's how you play the game."

Who?

Next comes "who?" This refers not only to the "who," the agent (the one acting), but also the "whom," the one acted upon. Identity and role add important dimensions to decisions. Who we are matters morally. Morality is not in the first instance about action but about the person who is the agent of action. Who we are spills over into what we do. Since we are all unique and different, asking "who?" makes us aware that what might be right for one person is wrong for another. Or what is right for you now (a student intern) may be wrong for you later (a licensed physician). Whether I am a diabetic or not affects the morality of my eating habits. Moreover, duties are entailed with our roles. A father is more responsible for the well-being of his children than is an uncle. If a person is conscientiously committed to nonviolence, it would be wrong for that person to take up arms in war. In medicine, how we communicate information to a patient will depend on who the patient is. We don't tell children the same kinds of things we tell an adult about his or her physical condition. No two persons are the same. Thus, it is unhelpful and wrong to bunch disparate people under one heading.

When? and Where?

The questions "when?" and "where?" locate the event in time and place. *When* something is done is morally important if timing is integral to the action. For example, when we pull the plug on life-support systems is morally significant. Does it happen before or after we have determined that any further treatment would be futile? Education in sexuality must be age appropriate if it is to lead to responsible behavior. To work overtime consistently so that fewer need to be employed when many people are out of work raises questions about justice for all. For a woman to smoke or to drink alcohol when she is pregnant would be morally objectionable. To wash down your driveway means one thing when the reservoirs are full and another thing when there is a drought. To be away from home for long periods of time means one thing when children are small and need parental presence and guidance; it means something else when children are more independent.

Where something happens is morally significant if location gives meaning to the action. For example, yelling "Fire!" in a crowded theater is morally different from yelling "Fire!" on a rifle range. Driving sixty-five miles per hour on an interstate highway is morally different from driving the same speed through the parking lot. Driving with a rifle slung across the rack of the back window of a pickup means something different in Montana and in Boston.

What If?

Consequences

"What if?" is the question of foreseeable effects. Some circumstances that influence the meaning of what we do lie in the future. If I choose this, what will result? The effects of our actions go beyond the present time and space and beyond those we intend to affect. Moral responsibility means that we ought to look as far into the future as we can to judge the impact of our behavior. A great moral failure is shortsightedness. We fail to look beyond the immediate good that we intend to the evil effects that we cause along with the good. Many of the effects of our actions are beyond our intention. Even though we are not morally responsible for all effects, we are responsible for those that we can and should foresee, even if we did not intend them. So we ought to anticipate as many effects as possible.

"What if?" cautions us from making decisions based only on intended effects or on not looking beyond tomorrow to the long-term and social consequences of our choice. A good example is *Ex* the ecological disasters of soil, air, and water pollution. People yet unborn should influence our analysis of what is right to do with the environment. Another example is the assisted-suicide debate. What if we establish it as a practice? What will that do to our quality of mercy? To the moral character of the medical profession? To the atmosphere that surrounds the debilitated, the elderly, the chronically ill? To our attitude toward them?

"What if?" forces us to calculate the good and bad effects with the other circumstances. In medicine, giving painkillers to shorten pain may also bring about the effect of hastening death. Deciding whether we can give the medication depends on other factors, such as who we are treating and when we are giving the medication. In our business life, what if we have a two-martini lunch with every prospective client? What if we use prescription drugs to settle tension caused by our work? Have we considered the dangers of addiction? Are we being blind to the real source of the tension that is often interpersonal and not biological?

What Else?

"What else?" forces us to unearth options. If we ignore realistic possibilities, then we are being deficient in our moral reflection. If we have no other avenues for action, then we have no real moral problem. The choice is simplified.

Exploring options demands a creative imagination. We often think too narrowly about what we can do and how. But in these days, when we constantly see the undoable being done in medicine, in space exploration, in technology, we ought to be alert to expanding our vision of ways to achieve a good end. What else can we do instead of using oil as our primary source of energy, of driving alone to work, of watching television as our primary source of entertainment, of working three jobs in order to maintain a luxuriant lifestyle, of putting our parents in a nursing home, of killing a lonely patient in a nursing home who wants to die, of taking pills for relief of tension, of capital punishment as our response to crime? Too often we make the wrong moral choice, not because we are bad people, but because we are too unimaginative.

Conclusion

These, then, are the reality-revealing questions that help us uncover morally relevant dimensions that define the situation to which we must respond. They help us appreciate the special context in which we find ourselves and to appreciate those features of our situation that make for a moral difference in shaping what we ought to do. But this situational analysis is not enough for discernment. We must still consider the person who is the moral subject of this process. For it is the person who is trying to hear

God's call in this situation and who must decide what is the most fitting way to express his or her fundamental commitment to God in this moment.

CRITICAL REFLECTION:

1. How does the above presentation on the situational context affirm your present approach to analyzing the situation? *I relearned that...*
2. What new insight did you gain from this chapter? *I was surprised to learn that...*
3. What questions does your new learning raise for you? *I need to think more about...*

APPROPRIATION:

1. Share an anecdote from your life that illustrates how situational analysis was important to your process of deciding what to do. *I remember when...*
2. How would you like to analyze the situation in the future? *Next time, I want to...*

5. Personal Context

- *What aspects of yourself as a moral agent do you pay attention to in deciding what to do?*
- *Which aspect of yourself is most influential in making a decision?*

ßⴰ

Finally, we come to the center of moral discernment, the person. This is a focus on the "I" of the practical moral question, "What ought I to do?" This is the person who is living in a social context and facing the reality of a situation calling for a response.

Everyday morality is largely a matter of character.[1] "Character" refers to that unique set of traits that "characterize" the kind of person one is and the actions one does. These "characteristics" are what we try to name in eulogies and in letters of recommendation. Moral character represents the persistent configuration of the beliefs, images, ideals, perspective, attitudes, dispositions, virtues, and vices from which our moral discernment and actions spring.

We act the way we do largely because the situations in which we find ourselves challenge us to reveal the beliefs we hold, the image we have of ourselves, the ideals we aspire to, our

85

perception of what is going on, the attitudes we have toward the realities we have to face, and the habits we have formed from persistent actions in the past. We reveal our character best when no one is looking to supervise us, to correct us, or to influence us. At those times we draw from our personal center to act in ways that reveal the stuff we are made of. This poem of an anonymous author expresses it well:

> Watch your thoughts; they become your words.
> Watch your words; they become actions.
> Watch your actions; they become habits.
> Watch your habits; they become character.
> Watch your character; it becomes your destiny.[2]

Central to our moral character is our fundamental stance, or the established point of view from which we interpret and evaluate our experiences. Two dominant but opposing points of view, for example, are those of the pessimist and the optimist. One sees the glass half empty; the other, half full. The pessimist looks on the world as ultimately meaningless and is prone to despair. Nothing has ultimate significance. The optimist, by contrast, sees the world as being sustained by a fundamental graciousness and so can live with hope, with an openness to surprise, with a sensitivity to change, and with a readiness to welcome something new.

Our basic stance in the world is shaped largely by committing our freedom to the way of life embodied in the communities that influence us with their tradition, stories, and images of the way life ought to be and by imitating the people within these communities who fascinate us with their style of life. Christian character develops to the extent that we commit ourselves to Christ and are informed by the stories and traditions that witness to his way of life. The church contributes to the development of Christian moral character through its direct moral teaching as well as by celebrating the sacred mysteries, telling the story of

Jesus, and witnessing to the faith and to moral truth in the way it lives to transform society according to the vision of the gospel.

Closely related to our basic stance or fundamental posture are our dispositions, our readiness to act in a certain way: lovingly or selfishly, courageously or fearfully, truthfully or deceptively. We commonly recognize dispositions as "habits of the heart," or virtues, when they enable us to fulfill the richest potential of human nature. We call them vices when they do not. Cultivating virtues is our way of cooperating with God's gift of the Spirit.

Our stance and dispositions pervade all aspects of the process of discernment. They affect how we interpret and evaluate what we see and the values we let predominate and how we interpret and apply principles and balance them against each other when they conflict. To understand our moral choices properly, then, we need to attend to aspects of our character. This chapter will examine those that especially influence the process of discernment.

Emotions and Intuitions

Moral awareness begins in the emotions and intuitions as an affective-intuitive reaction to a situation.[3] Emotions and intuitions are aspects of the personal context that are closest to our decisions. We begin with a gut reaction, a hunch. This is not a neutral outburst. Our emotions and intuitions give us an immediate, initial interpretive reaction to our situation before we begin critical, evaluative reflection of it. This reaction shows that we are not entirely ignorant of the moral dimensions of the situation. Feelings of anguish in the face of a severely handicapped newborn or excitement over sexual attraction or outrage at the violation of justice, for example, open us to the moral dimensions of experience and already represent a preliminary moral judgment. We are driven to get our rational analysis straight because we feel deeply about the values at stake and are already involved in a preliminary, precritical moral appraisal of what our responsibilities ought to be.

While an emotional reaction gives us a tentative signal that what we are experiencing is compatible with the dignity of persons or not, our intuition sees how the facts of the situation fall into a pattern and so help us make critical sense of it. The kind and intensity of the emotions that accompany our intuitions are a clue to what we stand for and how we will respond. An experience of delight when we see someone do a kindly deed, for example, is a response to a value that is congenial with our character and convictions. It can lead us to encourage, affirm, or reward the kind person. The feeling of anger evoked by an egregious act of injustice tells us that something does not fit what we stand for, and it moves us to set relationships right.

Only a completely rationalist view of the person and of morality would dismiss emotions and intuitions as bearers of moral information. Since we have inherited a tradition in ethics that has favored moral judgment as largely a matter of reason and since we live in a culture that is a child of rationalism where clarity of mind determines the value of experience, we ought not to be surprised to see a suspicious eyebrow raised at the thought of giving a place to emotions and intuition in the moral life. For rationalists, emotions only fog the mind and cloud moral judgment. The rationalist thinks that critical reflection is at war with the emotions and that the only trustworthy guide to moral wisdom is dispassionate, rational deliberation. To be objective, they say, is to be detached. To be careful in deliberation is to be cool, calm, and collected.

But if we get overly preoccupied with reason, we can forget that what causes us to see a moral problem in the first place is our emotional reaction to it. Feelings can guide our perception. They do not always have to distort it. Granted that our emotional reactions are subject to social conditioning and so need to be tested against broader experiences and critical reflection, these reactions can also enrich our experience and cause us to revise our positions. Distance and detachment do not always help us see clearly. Take, for instance, the love of a parent for a child or the care of a physician for a patient. The parent's "loving perception" or the physician's "felt concern" alerts each to subtle nuances in the child or the patient that disinterested detachment would never see.

But our moral training has rarely given attention to developing skills of emotional response. When, for example, do you recall ever being told to focus on the emotional feelings you have? Isn't it true that so much more of our moral training has focused on what we are obliged to do or prohibited from doing or on what intention or motivation we should have? Precious little in our moral education has been directed to the importance of acquiring the skills of emotional responses—feeling sad at the death of a loved one and offering condolence, feeling empathy toward the vulnerable and reaching out to help, feeling sympathy toward a colleague and offering support. Having appropriate feelings is an indispensable component of moral awareness. Just doing the right thing is not enough to be moral. Being moral also involves feeling appropriate emotions, not only love and sympathy but even anger and indignation. One who donates blood out of mere duty so that a family member can have surgery is less praiseworthy than the one whose help flows from concern and empathy for the sick relative.

Emotions and intuition are a way of knowing, even though these are prior to self-conscious, critical reflection. But please understand me. To recognize the role of emotion and intuition in making a moral decision does not make the moral choice simply an emotional reaction or a pure intuition. It does not lead to advocating "if it feels right, do it" as a moral guide. In fact, just as emotions and intuitions communicate their own insights, so they can perpetuate their own prejudices. To the extent that our emotions and intuitions have been influenced by the culture, they are not altogether dependable as truly personal guides. They may be misleading, biased, or wrong. While we need to trust them for the moral dimensions of experience they open to us, we need to distrust them for their potential to mislead us. For example, someone who is divided by chaotic emotions, smothered in shame, tortured by unhealthy guilt, or subject to frequent and severe mood swings will not be able to rely on emotions as a source of moral knowledge. A sound moral discernment, then, is never a purely affective evaluation; but neither is it purely cognitive. It blends both. Even though emotions and intuitions are not the whole of moral awareness and can be misleading, they are still important enough to listen to them. Together they prompt us to engage in the process of critical reflection and to draw upon other sources of moral information from our situational and social contexts. Affections unaided by disciplined reflection can lead to moral chaos; but reflection without affect leads nowhere. Since we feel more than we can explain, moral knowledge must include a discerning sensibility that cannot be fully explained.

Emotions and intuitions, then, are our first attempt to bridge the gap between what is going on and how we respond to it. Together they prompt us to look closer at our situation in order to see what else must be taken into account and what other interpretive patterns fit the facts of the case. They push the discernment process to the level of critically reflecting on what is going on and what we should do. When we finally try to express our reflected interpretation and evaluation, we do so in the language of principles, obligations, duties, or in the moral categories of right and wrong.

A truly reasonable moral choice, then, will be based on emotions, intuitions, faith, and reason working together. Reason defines the problem, gathers information, takes counsel with others, assesses the data, and turns to a larger frame of reference to bring clarity and coherence to it. While engaging this rational process, we need to pay attention to our intuitions and emotional reactions. When we intuit but can't explain why a line of reasoning is wrong, our emotions induce us to continue to look beyond the present arguments for an acceptable solution. We continue to let faith, reason, emotion, and intuition engage each other in a prayerful listening until we can bring all their voices into harmony.

When there is a conflict between strong emotional reactions and strong reasons, which way should we go? When there is such a tension, we cannot decide wholeheartedly. If we are the kind of person who has developed the habit of striving to seek the truth and to do what is right and if we are presently disposed in this manner, then if we must decide before the tension gets resolved, we ought to follow the tendencies of our personality that we have favored and developed to help us make decisions. This means that if we know ourselves to be more a right-brain (analytical) person than a left-brain (intuitive, affective) person, we ought to follow critical reason. But if we are more a heart person than a head person, we ought to follow our heart.

But if we do not have to decide until we can reach a harmony of faith, reason, emotion, and intuition, we would have a more reliable clue that we are moving in the right direction. If we choose in continuity with this harmony, we can have more confidence that we will be doing what we ought to do in loving response to God calling us in and through the situation.

Somatic Reactions

Closely aligned with emotions and intuitions are our bodily reactions, attesting the psychosomatic unity of the human person. Medical studies confirm that our emotions have far-reaching physical effects. But we still fail to take ourselves seriously as a unity and so miss the connections. I once heard it put humorously, but with some truth, that those who have hemorrhoids may be sitting on their feelings too much; those with migraines may be thinking about their feelings; those with nervous stomachs have swallowed too many feelings. While these may not be exact diagnoses, there is enough truth in them to pay attention to the connections between our emotions and our bodies.

Unfortunately, we miss the body's clues because so many of us suffer from some type of repressed bodiliness. We are simply out of touch with our bodies. When we do get in touch with them, we often can't find the language to talk about our bodily reactions. Yet we know that when we use expressions like "My skin crawled at the suggestion" or "I tingled when I saw a new possibility," there is a connection between how our bodies react and what fits us. If we ignore the body, then we are going to miss out on a valuable avenue to moral awareness.

While we engage the back-and-forth, round-and-about movement of faith, reason, emotion, and intuition and while we imaginatively walk around inside a possible choice in order to get face-to-face with the situation we will create by acting in a certain way, we need to pay attention to our bodily reactions. They will often be our early warning system that we are moving in the right direction or not. Symptoms indicating that we are moving in the wrong direction would be such reactions as a racing heart, unusual sweating, diarrhea, hemorrhoids, backaches, headaches, tightness in the neck and shoulders, stomach cramps, sleeplessness, persistent colds and coughs. Symptoms indicating that we are moving in the right direction are a feeling of being fully alive, bright, light, and free because we are in harmony.

Beliefs

Our emotions and intuitions rise to the surface prodded not only by the stimuli of a situation but also by our basic beliefs. By beliefs I mean our stable convictions.[4] These are the truths we live by, our heartfelt commitment to values that promote well-being. These convictions can be religiously grounded or not; they may be conscious or not. We become more conscious of the beliefs we live by as we confront a variety of situations calling for a response and as we examine the pattern of actions that make up our lives. The abortion debate, for example, awakens our convictions about the sanctity of life, the right to privacy, the limits of our freedom, and sexual responsibility. Debates over war and peacemaking invoke our convictions about the purpose of government and the use of force.

Our beliefs about the value of persons are so basic that they really drive our moral actions. One religiously grounded belief about the value of persons is that we are made in the image of God. Because of this conviction, we believe that there are certain ways that people ought to regard one another so that some choices are never truly open because they offend human dignity. For example, persons ought to be respected as ends and not used as means to be exploited for one's own gain. The belief that each person has dignity as a gift of God grounds the claim that each person is to be respected in every situation and in every type of activity as someone sacred and not because of that person's role in society, achievements, or attributes of intelligence, beauty, or skills.

Our beliefs about God also influence our moral choice, since we approach the moral life with God as our fixed point of reference, the source and goal of our moral striving. Our belief that God is creator, for example, engenders a sense of dependence upon one another and ultimately upon God. It engenders an attitude of living within the limits of our freedom as creatures and fostering good stewardship for all of creation. The central belief about God in the Christian faith is that God is love. To believe that we are made in the image of a God who is self-giving is to say that we are capable of self-gift in return.

We might have other beliefs as well that influence our moral choice. For example, we have certain beliefs about the way social roles ought to be fulfilled. We believe that parents ought to provide a nurturing environment for their children and physicians ought to tell us the truth about a diagnosis and prognosis. We also say that we believe that all persons are created equal. How do we let these beliefs influence the way we structure ourselves as a society?

We also have some basic convictions about who we are to be *for* one another and how we are to be *toward* one another. For example, if we equate our value with our work, we will drive ourselves to do more and do it better. If we believe that good Christians don't get angry, we will repress this emotion and never use its energy to set relationships right. If we believe that there ought to be peace at any price, we will devote our energies to avoiding conflict or to seeking reconciliation when conflict occurs. Our beliefs need to be examined to see if they are true to our Christian heritage and to healthy human living.

Imagination

Another important dimension of the personal context is the imagination.[5] What we decide to do is not as much motivated by our fundamental convictions and reasons as it is by our imagination. The imagination is the great instrument of moral good. Since we "see" the world through images and not otherwise, the imagination so defines who we are that we can get a clue to our moral character by recognizing the master images that dominate the imagination. This does not negate the importance of giving reasons for our actions, but it does remind us that our reasons will be convincing only if they are consistent with the world of images we are using to interpret our experiences.

By the imagination I do not mean a capacity for frivolity in an otherwise serious world. As a moral resource, the imagination is not a flight of fancy. It is the capacity to construct a moral world. By means of the imagination, we bring together diverse aspects of our experience into a meaningful whole. It is how we make sense of things. When we were children, we would look into the clouds and see faces, a horse, or a castle. We would make those random puffs of water vapor fit into a meaningful pattern by drawing upon images we had already collected from previous experiences. In the process of discernment, the imagination works in a similar way. It brings into a meaningful whole all the diverse parts we have acquired from examining the social and situational contexts.

Since what counts for us morally depends a great deal upon what we see, the images that dominate our imaginations are powerful moral resources for deciding what to do. Every teacher knows the power of an apt example, and every preacher knows the effect of a story well told. Frequently our students and congregations do not understand a simple point, not because they lack intelligence, but because they are looking in the wrong direction. A good example or a well-told story allows the listener to suspend prior judgment about the way things ought to be so that a new image may play. Suddenly all is clear: "Oh, I get the picture! I've just never seen it that way before!" When we "get the picture," we have come to an image that helps us put all the diverse parts together so that we can understand and respond appropriately. What we decide to do, then, becomes a function of the "picture" we have of the world. As we imagine, so we are and become and do.

The imagination contributes to discernment by both shaping what we see (an interpretive function of focusing our perception) and envisioning what is possible (a creative function empowering emotion, motivation, and intention). A few examples are in order to illustrate the way in which the metaphors or images through which we see and describe our world influence the way we act.

Consider health care. How often we use military metaphors to think about and to talk about medical cases! We look on physicians as commanders with an arsenal of powerful weapons—medicines, procedures, machines—to use on the battlefield of the patient's body in order to fight the enemy—disease and, above all, death. Within this military model of delivering health care, there is no room for questioning orders. Obedience is the only order of the day. The physician remains in charge. The patient only obeys.

Try a new metaphor now. What would the delivery of health care be like if we used the image of the physician and patient in covenant with each other sharing the responsibility to be stewards of limited resources? How different would the physician-patient relationship be then? What would happen to our attitude toward sickness and death?

Consider the debate over immigration. For some the Statue of Liberty is the controlling image to direct a policy that invites a compassionate response of hospitality. It is countered by the military images of immigrants as invaders who need to be repelled and of borders barricaded. These are only two examples, but I hope that they are enough to show that the images through which we see and the feelings they arouse influence the way we respond and the reasons we would find justifiable for our actions.[6]

The major issue related to the ethical function of the imagination is what voices and traditions we allow to influence us. My earlier discussions of the formation of conscience and of the communities of influence in the social context of discernment are relevant here. Most of what we see does not lie in front of our eyes but behind them in the images that fill our imaginations. We do not come to any situation like blank film in a camera ready to record whatever is there. Our film has already been exposed to frameworks of meaning fashioned by the images we have inherited from our social worlds.

Where do we get the primary images through which we interpret what is going on? Our imagination depends a great deal on our relationships. Social scientists tell us that the images that fill our imaginations are largely the result of the beliefs and values, causes and loyalties, of the communities that have the greatest influence on us. The images that come to us through the entertainment community often stand in direct conflict with the images of the gospel and rob religious stories and images of their power to move us. If we look on the world through the images of police dramas, situation comedies, and soap operas, we may see that violence and exploitation simply come with the territory of living together and that the young, strong, and beautiful are the ones who need loving. But if we look on the world through the images of covenant, creation, sin, incarnation, cross, and resurrection, for example, we see a different world. There people need one another and work together for the well-being of all. But if our imaginations are filled with images of war, greed, corrupt power, and exploitation, then we look on the world in a way that protects self-interest at the expense of everyone else.

Social scientists tell us that whoever controls the images controls society. We need to be aware of the image makers who provide us with the lenses through which we see the world. We need to be critical of the dominant images in our lives and where they come from. Who are the people who have captured our imaginations, what are the experiences that stand out as representing for us what life ought to be like?

In addition to helping us see, the imagination also helps us move into the future and create our world. So much of moral instruction is aimed at getting others to behave differently by trying to convert their wills. We try to reason with them, to preach at them, badger, or shame them into selflessness. But what is really at stake is not that they are stupid, selfish, closed, or uncaring. They simply lack imagination. They assume that what they are doing now is the only way to respond to a situation. They can't act any differently because they can't imagine what it would be like to be someone else.

If a possible way of acting is not perceived as being real, then we will never achieve it. Only if we can imagine a new way of life can we ever make it real for us. The bumper sticker that says Imagine Peace challenges us to imagine a world without war. If we can't, then we won't ever achieve it. There are many reasons not to act for justice, but the primary one is that we can't imagine what it should look like.

Good discernment requires imagination to recognize the complex web of responsibilities in a particular case, to entertain alternatives of action, and to anticipate different kinds of consequences. Good discernment also requires imagining what it would be like to be in the shoes of those affected by what we do.

So we need to nurture the imagination as an asset of discernment. We can do this by broadening our experiences through travel, literature, film, and cross-cultural and cross-generational conversations. Anything that will help us see more broadly and with more discrimination will aid discernment.

Prayer

If we are going to approach moral decisions as believers, then prayer is our indispensable context for discernment.[7] Without prayer it is hard to keep our love of God foremost in our consciousness. Without prayer this whole process of discernment becomes nothing more than a disciplined method for solving a problem.

Since discernment is the process of interpreting the patterns evoked by the interplay of faith, reason, emotions, and intuitions, it requires some "downtime" for these patterns to emerge. So that these patterns can present themselves with God's support, this downtime must be spent in faith in the context of prayer. The prayer of discernment is the attentive attitude and posture of openness to God's presence that provides the time and space for this to happen. It enables a plausible view of what is going on to emerge so that we can see what obligations and responsibilities are at stake in light of our fundamental commitment to God.

The prayer of discernment must take the form of listening, or paying attention, not only to what is going on outside us in the situation calling for a response but also to what is happening within us as we face the situation. The first steps in discerning are to identify and clarify what is going on in our experience and what feelings and somatic reactions are evoked in us by the experience. Only by means of attentive listening to these signals will we hear what God is calling us to do.

Prayerful openness to what is going on is also a way to free ourselves from external pressures and from selfish preferences that get fixed in advance on one particular option. With an interior freedom, we can leave ourselves open to the choice that truly expresses who we are and aspire to become and that is also truly responsive to the most pressing moral values in the moment.

For such a prayerful discernment, we need time, leisure, and quiet. We cannot look inward and listen when we are caught up in the hectic activity that forces us to focus our attention on what is happening outside us. Out of the quiet come hunches and intuitions that seem to appear as though from nowhere. But in order to get access to this resource from within, we need quiet, leisure, and time.

We also need to be in reasonable physical health and to have sufficient moral, spiritual, and psychological maturity, which gives us the critical self-awareness to avoid confusing a discerning judgment with our addictions and illusions. If we are distracted by physical distress or divided by chaotic emotions, mood swings, or other neurotic conditions, we will not be able to rely on our emotions, intuitions, and somatic reactions for reliable guidance. If we do not know what is going on with ourselves, we will not be able to hear God's call coming to us through our internal and external experiences. To the extent that we can check self-deception and touch the center of ourselves in truth, to that extent will we be able to hear the call of God in our experience.

These, then, are some of the aspects of our personal context to which we must attend in the process of discernment. To use these resources of moral information well, we need to have a sufficient degree of self-knowledge. The lack of self-awareness remains our greatest obstacle to a reliable discerning judgment.

Conclusion

Apart from those situations where certain ways of acting are clearly immoral, such as acts of murder, rape, genocide, and the like, considering the relevant aspects of the social, situational, and personal contexts of the less clear situations of conflict yields only a modest claim that we know what God is asking of us for now. We must always recognize the limits of the process and the limits of our own self-understanding. Only a system of tight syllogisms, which leave no room for the affective and intuitive, can guarantee greater certitude concerning incontrovertible premises. Discernment gives not logical but moral certitude; it can tell us that we are moving with great probability in the right direction.

The test of this process is not whether it solves urgent dilemmas but whether it allows us to examine the various aspects of moral experience so that we can make our habitual way of being and acting more responsive to the movement of God in our lives. Ultimately, the decision to do this or not to do that rests less on a logical conclusion of a syllogism and more on an aesthetic judgment of harmony with one's sense of self. We choose on the basis of what fits the kind of person we know ourselves to be and aspire to become. The feeling that something fits us will be judged ultimately by whether it delights us and brings a sense of wholeness. That sense of inner harmony and wholeness is the interior sign that we are responding to the grace of God in the moment. If we act according to the direction of these interior feelings, we can be fairly confident that we are acting according to what God is calling us to do.

This concludes my description of a model of moral discernment. What remains is to put this model into practice in the ministry of offering pastoral guidance. To that I turn in the next and final chapter.

CRITICAL REFLECTION:

1. How does the above presentation on the personal context affirm your present awareness of yourself as a moral agent? *I relearned that...*
2. What new insight did you gain from this chapter? *I was surprised to learn that...*
3. What questions does your new learning raise for you? *I need to think more about...*

APPROPRIATION:

1. Share an anecdote from your life that illustrates how your own personal resources were important to the way you decided what to do. *I remember when...*
2. How would you like to include your personal resources in the future? *Next time, I want to...*

III. Application

6. Pastoral Moral Guidance

PRESENT UNDERSTANDING:

- *How do you understand the pastoral responsibility of being a moral guide?*
- *What do you expect from someone to whom you turn for moral guidance?*

❧

Thus far in this book, we have examined the nature of the moral conscience and a model for discerning what we ought to do. I have tried to show that acting in conscience is the matter of exercising our ability to discern right from wrong. The process of discernment includes exploring the social, situational, and personal contexts of the moral issue confronting us. Only by being as thorough as we can be in our examination of the total moral reality can we discover how we ought to express ourselves as persons of faith fundamentally committed to God.

The model of discernment I have outlined presumes that serious moral decisions are made in dialogue. This last chapter will round out the treatment of discernment by addressing the pastoral responsibility of providing moral guidance. In light of the previous discussion about discernment and acting in conscience, what does pastoral moral guidance look like? What can one expect from a moral guide? How might one offer moral guidance in a way consistent with the model of discernment just presented?

To develop my model of moral guidance, I will first distinguish between the objective pole of morality, which moral theology seeks to name, and the subjective pole of a person's capacity for knowing and doing what is right and avoiding what is wrong. This level has been the primary interest of this book, and it is the level a sensitive pastoral moral guide needs to honor. After distinguishing these two poles of morality, I will offer some suggestions for exercising effective pastoral ministry in the midst of theological pluralism. Finally, I will offer a model of pastoral moral guidance and illustrate it by constructing a dialogue about giving advice.

Moral Theology and Pastoral Guidance

The Catholic moral and pastoral traditions honor the distinction between *ought* and *can,* or the objective and subjective poles of morality. Both are real and important. But we must not confuse them, substitute one for the other, collapse one into the other, or compromise the objective order in the name of making allowances for human weakness. The typical way of confusing these poles is to say that what makes an action morally right or wrong is the way one thinks about the action in the situation at hand. On the contrary, the objectively right action is that which truly fits human nature. The subjectively right is what we truly believe to be fitting in this situation, even though we may be wrong. The goal of forming conscience and acting morally is to have the subjective discernment of what to do coincide with the requirements of objective moral standards.

In the following passage, Pope John Paul II also makes it quite clear that the subjective and the objective poles must not be confused:

It is quite human for the sinner to acknowledge his weakness and to ask mercy for his failings; what is unacceptable is the attitude of one who makes his own weakness the criterion of the truth about the good, so that he can feel self-justified, without even the need to have recourse to God and his mercy. An attitude of this sort corrupts the morality of society as a whole, since it encourages doubt about the objectivity of the moral law in general and a rejection of the absoluteness of moral prohibitions regarding specific human acts, and it ends up by confusing all judgments about values. (*VS,* 104)

"Ought" expresses the objective pole of morality. This imperative is what ethical reflection tries to uncover. Such reflection yields statements of right and wrong, such as "euthanasia is wrong" and "keeping promises is right." "Can" expresses the subjective pole of a person's capacity to choose right or wrong. This is the area that pastoral guidance needs to respect.

According to this distinction, the objective pole of morality refers to the way life ought to be lived in order to achieve the well-being of persons and the community. To uncover this objective order, we must ask, "What sort of persons ought we to be—despite our tendency to conflict and sin—and what sorts of actions ought we to perform in response to God's call to be loving?" Or "What are the demands of discipleship for today?" Or "What does it mean to be a good person, and what does a flourishing community look like?" Objective morality is the world of value that we must confront in making decisions. In this world, we include being truthful and compassionate, honest and chaste, courageous and respectful of life, property, and privacy. The world of objective morality is like the polestar on a journey. It keeps us fixed on moving in the right direction.

The Catholic moral tradition claims that the objective order of morality is in God's eternal plan for us. We can discover it through what God has revealed in Jesus (with the help of faith) and through what we can know by reflecting on the experience of being human (with the help of reason, or natural law). To claim that there is an objective standard of the way things ought to be doesn't guarantee that discovering the standard will always be easy or even that there will be one and only one right answer to every dilemma. Try as many people might, the moral life cannot be reduced to black and white. If that were the case, I wouldn't have had to go to such lengths describing moral discernment as the process for discovering the right thing to do in response to God's presence and action in the world.

Pastoral moral guidance, by contrast to moral theology, is the art of the possible. It focuses primarily on the subjective pole of morality, or the individual's conscience, rather than on abstract principles. The subjective pole of morality has to do with the behavior that flows from one's capacity of knowledge, freedom, and emotion to appreciate moral values, to commit oneself to them, and to choose them freely. Pastoral guidance is concerned with the ability of a person to fulfill the objective moral order. In other words, it seeks the best possible expression of basic human goods that this person can make at this time to satisfy what love demands. "Love one another as I have loved you" is a norm for life and so must be followed constantly. But there is a limit to what can be done by each person at each time in order to live truthfully, compassionately, and respectfully of self and others. To refuse to accept this is to demand perfect love from imperfect creatures. To face the reality of human sinfulness and to accept our limited ability to love is not to dissolve the gospel demand but to recognize that we are still in need of conversion. We are still on the way to the full flowering of love.

Pastoral guidance assesses a person's capacity by asking, "To what extent are you able to appropriate and choose (i.e., have the knowledge, freedom, and emotional stability for) a way of life that fulfills what love demands?" And "Given where you are, what is the next step you can take toward the ultimate good of living according to God's call to be loving?" In this way, pastoral guidance is directed toward the best possible moral achievement of the person for now, while encouraging and supporting the person's openness and growth toward living the fullness of love. The attitude of the one seeking guidance is to be open to conversion and moral growth. The pastoral guide must first nurture that growth by helping the other see where he or she still needs to go and identify the obstacles that lie between here and there and then help the person overcome those obstacles.

Traditionally, pastoral guidance follows the *principle of gradualism*. This means that a person progresses one step at a time toward a deeper integration of the demands of objective morality. For example, we may not be able to fulfill the demands of justice, honesty, truthfulness, chastity, and courage immediately. The pastoral moral guide must pay attention to what limits a person's ability to fulfill moral standards because of where that person may be in his or her moral development or because of the impediments to his or her freedom. Each person moves toward the fullness of being loving only at the pace and to the extent that he or she can. The sensitive moral guide needs to respect the dynamic of conversion at work in a person's moral growth. The principle of gradualism is the basis for treating with compassion those who are not yet able to realize all that love may require of them.

Both moral theology and pastoral guidance seek moral truth, or who we ought to be and what we ought to do in response to God's call to be loving. But moral theology does so apart from considering any particular individual person's situation of conflict and sin. Pastoral guidance, by contrast, takes the person and the situation into consideration in determining the good that can be achieved for now.

Therefore, appropriate pastoral guidance does not abandon objective morality when a person is unable to measure up to it, giving way to the soft-hearted sentiment that anything goes. But neither does pastoral guidance use objective morality as a club to beat others into submission to objective norms. Pastoral guidance always holds in tension the objective norms of morality (such as we would find in the teaching of the church) and the particular person's capacity for responsibility. In this way, a pastoral judgment is always related to normative standards and subject to them, but one is not collapsed into the other. By helping the other to reflect on where one is now in light of where we ought to be, the pastoral guide maintains the tension necessary for moral growth.

I hope that this explanation of a classic distinction in Catholic theology between normative moral order and pastoral practice that attends to the subjective order of conscience sheds some light on a common dilemma of pastoral ministers. How often I have had students phrase their dilemma like this, "How can I fulfill my professional responsibility as a formal representative of the church and faithfully uphold the moral teaching of the church (the sphere of normative moral theology) while, at the same time, honoring the struggle of those who are sincerely trying to live up to that teaching but are not yet able to integrate it in its fullness (the sphere of pastoral guidance)?" While the task of forming conscience is to bring together the moral rightness and subjective discernment of an issue, the task of moral guidance is to enable another to recognize and to choose for him or herself what is, in truth, the best course of action.

An index of maturing in one's role as a pastoral moral guide is the ability to hold in tension the objective and subjective poles of morality without collapsing one into the other. To sharpen the point, to serve as a moral guide, we need the sensitivity to distinguish between the good that ought to be (as expressed in the objective normative statement of morality) and the good that can only be achieved for now (a pastoral judgment based on one's limited subjective capacity to choose what is objectively best).

Good pastoral practice has traditionally held that *ought* implies *can*. This means that we are not to require a particular obligation in practice, however justifiable it may be theoretically, if the person cannot, for good reason, perform it. While everyone is always required to do what he or she can, no one is ever required to do what is beyond his or her reach. The preeminent Catholic moral theologian of this century, Bernard Haring, reflects the wisdom of St. Alphonsus Liguori, the patron of moral theologians, in giving this pastoral advice: "One should never try to impose what the other person cannot sincerely internalize, except the case of preventing grave injustice toward a third person."[1] We are accountable for doing what is within our capacity, and we are morally culpable for failing to do what we are capable of doing. While the situation may demand a certain kind of response objectively speaking (such as an accident victim's needing assistance), not everyone is capable of meeting the demands of the situation (two paramedics come upon the scene, but one is so emotionally traumatized as to be unable to respond). So two people facing the same situation can have different degrees of moral responsibility toward it.

Ministering in the Midst of Pluralism

Pastoral ministers today find themselves in the midst of diverse thinking on moral matters. So when it comes time to serve as a moral guide, they are often confused by sometimes conflicting voices. They find themselves in the situation of the helmsman in Herman Wouk's *The Caine Mutiny*. At one point in the action, a terrifying typhoon lashes the ship and the commanding officer, Captain Queeg, is thought to be too ill to command the ship responsibly. The executive officer goes to relieve Queeg of his duties, but Queeg sends him away and orders the helmsman to "come left to 180 degrees." But the executive officer yells to the helmsman, "Steady as you go!" The helmsman hears both commands: to turn left 180 degrees and to go straight ahead. Confused, he yells out, "What the hell should I do?" The helmsman is trained to follow orders of those he respects, but he is now getting conflicting orders from two responsible sources. To whom does he listen?

As I have already tried to show, one is always bound to follow the judgment of a properly formed conscience. The informing takes place in a community where we hear many voices, each claiming to be a source of moral wisdom. As my discussion of the social context of discernment tried to show, for Catholics the magisterium is a source of moral authority that is not simply one voice among many but normative. Pastoral ministers must offer guidance in light of magisterial teaching to those who struggle with it. How can the pastoral minister be faithful to the teaching of the church and still be mindful that he or she is presenting it to responsible people who also hear other voices of wisdom and must ultimately decide what to do in light of what they sincerely believe is right?

I want to offer a "survivor's guide" for ministers giving moral guidance in the midst of theological and moral pluralism.

1. Know your model of ministry as moral guide.

For so long the teaching role in and of the church had been conceived in juridical terms, with command/obedience as the dominant characteristic. The teaching of the church in disciplinary matters of law as well as in doctrinal and moral matters was treated as apodictic directives. According to this model, the mission of our ministry was to give answers by fitting the proper teaching (command) to the situation. It was that simple. No wonder so many people still approach us thinking that moral teaching is about enunciating rules, making moral decisions is knowing how to apply the rules, and moral living is about obeying rules. This approach to moral guidance often led to external conformity but not to an internalizing of the values that lie behind the rules. Even less did it encourage the further step of developing a relationship with Jesus, accepting his message, and emulating his style.

Today we are trying to see that our ministry as moral guides is more evangelical than juridical. Serving as a moral guide is integral to the proclamation of the gospel. In this evangelical model of ministry, moral teaching invites a response more than it commands obedience. We try to assimilate teaching and to live by it because we are truly convinced of the truth it presents. The evangelical model of moral guidance believes that moral responsibility goes far beyond conforming to detailed instructions. It believes that responsibility arises out of internalized convictions. But for anyone to act in such a responsible way in light of the teaching of the church, he or she must first be able to grasp the truthfulness of the teaching. To enable this to happen, the teaching must be explained and the learner must be open to it.

2. Know the teaching of the church.

To explain the teaching, we must first know it ourselves. In the evangelical model of ministry, the proclamation of truth demands that we make the teaching accessible in a sympathetic way. In matters of morality, this does not mean that we serve up a checklist of moral principles. We must remember that principles are summary statements of rich moral experience and theological reflection. In addition to knowing principles, we also need to be able to retrieve as best we can the experience and reflection that surround them so that we can demonstrate the validity and wisdom of the teaching that mediates these principles.

Furthermore, when we present the teaching, we ought to try to express its substance more than simply repeating its formulation. We do not fulfill our professional responsibility to present the teaching of the church by merely parroting a council document, the catechism, or an encyclical. In some instances, the formulations of teaching can obscure more than they reveal. For example, to answer the question "How are we to respond to church teaching?" with "We are to accept the teaching and adhere to it with a religious assent of soul" (*Lumen Gentium,* n. 25) is a true answer, but it is a summary answer that needs to be explained. The traditional teaching on ordinary and extraordinary means is another good example. The Vatican Declaration on Euthanasia recognized that, as a principle, this still holds good. But its meaning is less clear today because of the imprecision of the terms. The declaration suggests that perhaps "proportionate" and "disproportionate" means may be a better expression to capture the substance of the principle. In any case, we need to find the language and images that communicate best to the person seeking guidance from the teaching.

Included in the responsibility of knowing the teaching of the church is the responsibility to clarify the binding character of a particular teaching. *Lumen Gentium,* n. 25, and canons 749 to 753 affirm the traditional position that the magisterium commits itself to its teachings in different degrees so that different levels of assent to those teachings are required. The U.S. bishops' pastorals on nuclear war and the economy have helped us appreciate that a teaching of a general principle has more weight than a proposal for its practical application. These letters recognized that in making an application of principles, a prudential judgment is involved based on specific circumstances. So we can expect a certain diversity of outcomes even though we are using the same principles. In moral teaching, if we fail to distinguish principles from application, we overly commit the magisterium in a harmful and embarrassing way, we risk damaging the credibility of the magisterium, and we mismanage the appropriate pastoral use of moral teaching.

Presenting the teaching of the church also respects the weight of a teaching relative to the kind of document in which it appears and to the level of the magisterial source from which it comes. We have to realize that most of the time, our people are going to hear about some teaching of the church from a journalistic source before they hear it from us. Unfortunately, journalists who report religious news show little awareness of the subtle distinctions among church documents and their relative authoritative weight. When we read a headline such as "The Vatican declares...," we can be sure that the fine distinctions that identify the authoritative weight of the document and the statements within it are lost to the public. So we need to assume the responsibility of making the distinctions honored by our tradition.

The context in which we make these clarifications and distinctions is also very important. Many times I have heard people complain that they never hear anything about these distinctions from their ministers. "Why don't we hear this from the pulpit?" they ask. I say that I am glad that they don't hear about them in that setting, for that is not the purpose of a homily. The homily is to draw on the liturgical texts to interpret peoples' lives. The genre of a homily does not lend itself to treating controversial moral issues or doctrinal matters. So the pulpit is not the place from which to present this matter. A classroom of an adult education program is better. But even there significant differences in background and stages of faith invite misunderstanding and misuse of the material. A one-to-one setting may be the best place to tailor a presentation on this matter, but we simply can't take the time to give everyone such special attention. So we will have to do the best we can with our educational programs and then deal with the more serious difficulties in private.

3. Be familiar with the theological debate surrounding a teaching.

When there is theological debate surrounding a particular issue, we ought to acknowledge as much and try to represent it fairly. To do so is not encouraging "cafeteria Catholicism." We must remember, every magisterial teaching reflects a theological position. So we ought to remain conversant with theological discussions so that we can understand the position taken by the magisterium and the reasons offered in support of the position. Although Catholic theology recognizes the special gift of the Spirit in the magisterium and so speaks of a presumption in its favor, the church also recognizes that God's Spirit is moving through the community, including the spheres of moral theology, pastoral ministry, and the "sense of the faithful." Conscience is formed in the whole church, and so these other spheres can be helpful sources for people to use in trying to clarify their understanding of church teaching and to appropriate it.

But in presenting the theological discussion, we need to be clear that we are presenting matters of opinion. We ought not to confuse theological opinion and personal opinions with the official teaching of the church. When we are asked, "What does the church say about…," we ought to represent the teaching in a sympathetic manner. If we are asked our own opinion or that of theologians, we can give it as long as we distinguish what is opinion from what is official teaching.

These are my three suggestions for surviving as a pastoral minister called upon to give moral guidance in a world marked by pluralism. They do not guarantee that you will never be misunderstood or become the object of criticism. But they do represent solid features of our Catholic theological tradition upon which we can draw to give ourselves guidance and stability in a sometimes chaotic world.

A Model of Moral Guidance

Now that we have examined the difference between the objective pole of morality sought by moral theology and the subjective pole of the moral agent seeking pastoral guidance and have clarified fundamental responsibilities of a pastoral minister serving in the midst of moral pluralism, we are ready to sketch a model of pastoral moral guidance. How can we be true to the norms of objective morality and still respect the limited capacity of a person to appropriate those norms and live by what they demand? I want to suggest a model of giving moral guidance that is structured on the basis of three creative imperatives: let there be understanding, let there be encouragement, let there be challenge.

1. Let There Be Understanding!

Our ultimate goal in providing moral guidance is to enable others to act in good conscience, that is, to live authentically according to what they believe is morally true so that they stand in right relationship with God. The Catholic moral tradition has been outstanding in the way it has upheld the primacy of conscience. Each person is responsible for answering the call of God at the depth of his or her being. As I tried to show in the first chapter, each person is responsible for forming a right conscience, and one acts in conscience only when acting with knowledge, in freedom, and with emotional stability.

Our first task in offering moral guidance is to create an atmosphere in which those seeking guidance feel safe, accepted, and honored. We listen to understand, not in order to convert others to our way of thinking, but in order to enable them to act in good conscience.

One of the ways of letting there be understanding is to listen without blame or judgment. What do we listen for? We listen for what others expect of us. What they expect often reflects their attitude toward authority. Some come to us wounded by the misuse of authority in the past. They may be defensive, suspicious, or feel that anyone who represents the church must certainly be out of step with the times. Yet there is something about the church that brings them back to draw on its tradition and its vision for guidance. We must be gentle with them.

Others may come with little to no respect for their own authority so they have unreal expectations of us. These are the ones who expect us to have the answer, to be all-knowing, always to be there when they need us, and ultimately to tell them what to do. We must resist the temptation and the invitation to be paternalistic with them.

Still others have learned to trust their own authority. They don't need to be told what to do, but they want to draw on us for clarity and for a broader vision so that they can take charge and give direction to their life in a more informed way. We must respect their freedom and dignity.

When we hear clearly what others expect of us, then we can be clear about what we can offer them. Perhaps it is information that they need, or someone to clarify their conflict, or someone to offer a religious interpretation of what is happening to them. But if we don't listen, we won't be able to serve them in a way that enhances their knowledge, freedom, or emotional stability. Without these, there is little likelihood that they will be able to act in conscience.

When we have given others a safe space to tell their story and the dilemma they face, they may uncover what they truly believe and care about with heartfelt commitment. For those seeking guidance, the present moral conflict is of a piece with other experiences, pressures, and choices. By helping them to see this situation within the context of the larger story of their lives, they can come to a more critical understanding of the sort of persons they have become, the moral strength and limitations with which they must work, and the direction in which their lives have been moving.

2. Let There Be Encouragement!

Since the primary responsibility of a decision belongs to the one making it, we ought to be concerned that he or she is making as honest a decision as possible. We can be encouraging of this end to the extent that we help others to recognize their values and to accept their moral character and the direction they want their lives to take. We can also help them to see patterns that have emerged in their lives as a result of prior choices. Well-established patterns are a sign that we hold to certain convictions, that we have been building a certain character, and that we have established a basic commitment to a certain way of life. People take time to think through a moral decision and seek counsel in doing so because they want to set a clear and purposeful direction for themselves. This direction is generally a further development of the basic moral identity they have already achieved.

One way to let there be encouragement is by helping people set goals: Who do you want to become? What are you trying to achieve here? How do you want to get there? By helping people understand themselves better and set goals, we will be encouraging them to discern more carefully who they want to become and what they want to do. Remember that moral growth only happens when we take our own steps in our own way. Others may point out a direction for us, but if we don't ultimately choose that way for ourselves, then we are not making any moral progress. Not until we can acknowledge and accept our limitations and our strengths will we possess our own moral capacity and be able to take the next step toward God's call to be loving.

3. Let There Be Challenge!

We can't stop with simply encouraging others to be conscientious, since sometimes a sincere judgment of conscience can bring great harm to others. If one is about to do harm to others, we need to use all the moral persuasion we can to prevent that from happening. Sometimes we might even have to intervene directly, or appeal to lawful authorities to intervene, in order to prevent others from inflicting harm on innocent parties.

More often than not, our challenge will come in the form of calling the other to conversion by raising larger questions (whose interest is being served here? what kind of community will this make?), appealing to another set of values or principles (the common good over autonomy), invoking moral absolutes (murder, stealing), reframing the situation by means of another image (covenant over contract), or holding up as examples the lives of morally virtuous people (Thomas More, Mother Teresa) so that the one seeking guidance can become more self-critical and self-directing.

Another way that we can be challenging is by making distinctions where there are true differences. We all like to argue from analogy by comparing cases. But not all aspects of our comparative cases are really analogous. We need to recognize the differences. Moreover, too many times people want a simple answer to a complex question. Passing over the complexities of the case with a simple rule is not helpful. It avoids the challenge of critical reflection and too easily settles for pat answers in a world of complex shades of gray.

We can challenge critical thinking, too, by unearthing more of the "what if?" and "what else?" involved in every possible choice. These are the kinds of questions that make one think more deeply about the course of action one might want to pursue. Remember, more often than not we make the wrong choice not because we are unthinking but because we are just too unimaginative.

Giving Moral Guidance

Over the years, when I have asked pastoral ministers in what areas of life their moral guidance is sought, they name issues in health care more than any other, even sex. The issue especially troublesome is that of trying to decide whether to treat or not to treat a patient in a seriously compromised condition. I have constructed here into one dialogue a composite case of such a health care dilemma in order to illustrate what pastoral moral guidance might look like.

In this case, Mary is responsible for all decisions pertaining to the treatment of her husband, John. She is now facing a hard decision about his future treatment and wants to make a responsible decision guided by the Catholic medical-moral tradition. She approaches the pastoral care (PC) department for help.

PC: Hello, Mary. I understand you asked to see me.

MARY: Yes. I need some help with a decision I have to make about my husband.

PC: Can you review his situation for me?

MARY: We have been married for fifty-five years. John is now eighty-seven. I am eighty. We have cared for each other through our whole life together. John has always been a very handsome man, dignified, and a sharp thinker. But about seven years ago or so, he began to slip. Now I realize that he was showing early signs of Alzheimer's disease. He would forget names, even mine. He would forget where he was going or where he was and things like that.

Our children are grown now and live quite a distance, so I am left with his total care. Over the past five years, he has had a series of strokes that have caused some paralysis. This has made it impossible for him to speak anymore and to take care of himself in even simple matters. He is incontinent and his intellectual functions are hardly evident. Two years ago it got too much for me to take care of him. I simply couldn't manage him anymore, so I had to place him in the nursing home run by the Sisters of Mercy. It was hard to do that, but I really couldn't manage on my own anymore.

At the home, he sleeps most of the time, and for the past six months has been going in and out of a coma. But I still visit him every day. I tried to feed him as long as he could take sufficient food by mouth. Even with liquefied food, he would still frequently choke. They have had to place a tube through his nose and into his stomach so that he could be nourished. He has been this way for the past six months.

He is practically totally oblivious to his surroundings. In fact, I don't think he even knows I am there with him every day. He continues to pull at his tube and make groaning sounds as though he is uncomfortable. Now the doctor tells me that his throat is so irritated from pulling at the tube, that they are going to have to do surgery to place the tube directly into his stomach. Here is my problem. Do I really have to give them permission to do this? Can't we just take out the tubes and give him whatever he can take by mouth and stop putting him through this misery with surgery and more tubes?

PC: Oh, this is a difficult decision. Of all the decisions we have to make about terminating treatment, decisions about stopping medically assisted fluids and nutrition put our understanding and principles to the greatest test. Our natural instincts are that we ought to feed other people, no matter their condition.

To help you think through this issue, let's begin with what John would have thought about doing this. Ideally, John is the one to whom we would turn for this decision. But since he is not capable of deciding, you will have to. That certainly is a tough position to be in. I am sure that you want to make this decision in the same loving way that you have cared for him thus far. You have to ask yourself, "If John could speak to us now, what would he say in this situation?"

MARY: Even though he never said specifically what he would want done in a case like this, I think that I know what he would say now. We talked about writing one of those advance directives, but we never got around to it. But I remember that we did talk about the Karen Quinlan case a lot and how difficult the decisions were for her family. John said clearly then that he would never want to be prolonged the way she was. "Pull the plug" was his position on using those machines. So I think that he would say that he doesn't want us to continue with this treatment.

But I don't want to kill him. I simply don't see any
sense in prolonging this miserable way of life either. He
just lies there going in and out of a coma. He doesn't
relate to anyone in any meaningful way. I don't know
how anyone could say that he is experiencing any benefit beyond mere survival by prolonging his life this way.
If we can stop the use of a ventilator, why can't we stop
the use of these feeding tubes? Just because we have
them available to us, do we have to use them?

PC: That is precisely what we must decide. Certainly, the
availability of a treatment is no moral mandate to use it. I
am happy to hear that at least you have talked about a
similar case, though not identical, to John's. That you can
guess what he would want on the basis of his reaction to
the Quinlan case will be helpful in making this decision
for him. Many people have given some thought to stopping treatment when an invasive machine, such as a ventilator, has to be used. But few people include in their
thinking the thought of using feeding tubes. Not everyone would put feeding tubes in the same category as a
ventilator. So we do have to be a little careful about treating them exactly alike. Remember, Karen Quinlan was in
a permanent vegetative state but continued to breathe on
her own after they removed the ventilator. She survived
in that condition for about ten more years. John is not in a
permanent vegetative state. He goes in and out of a coma,
and he cannot take sufficient food by mouth. If you agree
to remove John's feeding tubes, he is not going to eat
enough on his own to survive for very long.

Most everyone agrees that the use of a ventilator is a
form of medical treatment. But not everyone feels the
same way about medically assisted nutrition and hydration. Some people with whom I have spoken about this
issue have very strong visceral reactions to withdrawing
medically assisted fluids and nutrition. In the professional literature there has been quite a debate on this
issue. It is not hard to understand why, either. Not to use

feeding tubes, in whatever form, seems to go against our basic instincts to care for one another.

MARY: But doesn't the *way* we are feeding him matter, and not just *that* we are doing it? Surely how we are doing something must make a difference? Remember, John has been kept alive by means of medical technology, even if it is only that tube through his nose and into his stomach. Do we have to put him through surgery so that we can switch the tube and place it directly into his stomach?

PC: That's a very good observation, Mary. Some would say that how we go about this feeding is morally significant. You see, in the debate on this topic, some have claimed that merely providing the nutrition is the key moral feature. For them the method is irrelevant. They see withholding the nutrition as a failure to care and the wrong thing to do. Others say that, while that is generally true, the fact that nutrition is provided by means of some technical assistance and not by hand is the crucial moral factor. Under this view, it would be acceptable to stop the medical assistance, especially when the method being used seems to cause John so much discomfort and does not offer him any prospects for improving.

MARY: Before John had those strokes, he was able to feed himself, even though that didn't make any difference to his mental abilities. He was still pretty much out of it when it came to remembering or trying to have a conversation with him. The doctors told me that there was nothing that could be done to restore his mental capacities.

PC: Yes, Mary, and even though you knew John was mentally impaired and would not get better, you continued to provide him the food he needed. You didn't question whether that was the right thing to do then. It was not until the means of feeding him began to cause him misery that you began to ask whether there are grounds for stopping it. Isn't that true?

MARY: Yes. I don't want to impose on him a form of caring or treatment, or whatever you want to call it, that really isn't going to do any good. I think that we ought to consider whether this treatment is really beneficial or not.

PC: You are certainly on the right track and in line with the Catholic tradition by focusing on benefits. A long-standing tradition of Catholic moral teaching has recently been confirmed by the U.S. bishops in their 1994 *Ethical and Religious Directives for Catholic Health Services.* These are the most official guidelines for directing Catholic health care services in this country. The moral framework of these guidelines has been supported by Pope John Paul II in his 1995 encyclical *The Gospel of Life (Evangelium Vitae).* This is the highest authoritative source to which Catholics can appeal for direction in matters pertaining to the proper care of human life.

This core teaching in the Catholic tradition has given rise to several moral principles. Some of the ones pertinent to John's case are that our duty to preserve life is not absolute, that the well-being of the whole person must be taken into account in deciding about treatments, that we have the right to refuse life-prolonging treatments that are not sufficiently beneficial but are overly burdensome, and that we must never intend to kill another, though we may sometimes allow someone to die.

MARY: I am more familiar with the notion of ordinary and extraordinary means. I thought that this was the Catholic teaching. Wouldn't it apply to John's case?

PC: It certainly does. The ordinary/extraordinary distinction is one of the great contributions of the Catholic moral tradition to health care ethics. Its commonsense realism has been widely adopted in this field. The problem with it, however, is the way people understand it. The incorrect use of the distinction is to focus on the treatment itself. Those who do this conclude that feeding tubes are always ordinary means and so must be used because they are readily available, easy to use, low risk, and achieve the medical goal of getting nutrition into the body.

But the way the Catholic tradition has used the distinction is to focus, not only on the means of treatment, but also on the effects the treatment will have on the patient. The distinction helps us focus on the benefits and burdens that would result for this patient if the treatment were to be used. We say that any treatment that would be insufficiently beneficial or too burdensome for this patient would be extraordinary. What makes the treatment extraordinary is that the patient is in an extraordinary condition, namely, unable to benefit from any further treatment.

Because of the imprecision of the terms "ordinary" and "extraordinary," the 1980 Vatican Declaration on Euthanasia recognized that some people prefer to speak of "proportionate" and "disproportionate" means. This distinction helps us focus on the effects on the patient rather than consider just the treatment itself. It suggests that we ask "proportionate to what?" The answer is "proportionate to the benefits the patient would gain from the treatment over the burdens that result." The declaration makes it quite clear that it is morally permissible to withdraw treatments when "the techniques applied impose on the patient strain or suffering out of proportion with the benefits which he or she may gain from such techniques" (IV). We always assess the benefits and burdens from the patient's perspective. We want to know if he or she would be helped more than hurt by the proposed treatment.

MARY: So my decision about whether to allow the surgery really comes down to weighing the benefits and burdens of the treatment from John's perspective as best as I can know that.

PC: Yes. That is what we are always doing when we decide to treat or not to treat. In your case it is especially perplexing because we are dealing with a proposed treatment that will provide nutrition that will sustain John's physical life. You have to ask questions like, If we use this treatment, at what level of physical and mental functioning will it restore John's life? For how long? At what cost? How much discomfort will he have? How will it affect me? If we don't use the surgery and the tubes, what kind of discomfort will he have as a result of the lack of adequate nutrition and hydration? What else can we do to keep him comfortable? What makes this decision especially tough is that we feel that feeding is a basic act of caring. Who would ever want to say, "Don't feed!" That is so cruel.

MARY: But I am not saying, "Don't feed." I am saying, "No tubes." We will have to do the best we can with oral feeding. I don't think that merely sustaining his physical life serves his total well-being. Because of his dementia, paralysis, and being in and out of a coma, he doesn't have any way to achieve any other values beyond physical life, and that is seriously compromised. He can't relate to anyone in any meaningful way, and the continued care that he demands is taking its toll on me. Doesn't that count, too?

PC: Yes. All of your considerations count. The Catholic tradition is not a vitalist tradition that says that we must maintain physical life at all costs as long as we have the means to do so. No. Our position is to consider the person holistically. We are concerned with the totality of the person's life, not just with breathing or digesting. In fact, the U.S. bishops have declared as much in their directives: "No person should be obliged to submit to a health procedure that the person has judged, with a free and informed conscience, not to provide a reasonable hope of benefit without imposing excessive risks and burdens on the patient or excessive expense to family or community" (*ERD,* n. 32). And then, "The well-being of the whole person must be taken into account in deciding about any therapeutic intervention or use of technology. Therapeutic procedures that are likely to cause harm or undesirable side-effects can be justified only by a proportionate benefit to the patient" (*ERD*, n. 33). Pope John Paul II spoke in a like manner when he said that the duty to allow oneself to be cared for must be determined on the basis of whether "the means of treatment available are objectively proportionate to the prospects for improvement" (*EV*, n. 65).

These statements show rather clearly that we can forgo any treatment that does not offer reasonable hope of benefit or entails excessive burden. In our tradition, we have not equated the hope of benefit with merely sustaining physical life. Benefit ought to include a reasonable state of well-being. We have traditionally interpreted the burdens rather broadly. For example, we have included the physical burdens of pain and inconvenience; the psychological burdens of fear, of repugnance, of overly restricting one's freedom for preferred activities, or of the emotional drain on the caregivers. We have also included the economic burden of costs to family and community and the social burdens of using resources of the community.

MARY: But are you sure all of this applies to feeding tubes? Aren't they really in a category of their own? It seems that everything you have said makes sense when we are thinking about large, complicated, invasive, and expensive treatments such as the use of a ventilator, dialysis, amputations, and complex surgery. But what about simple surgery and feeding tubes?

PC: It is difficult to conceive of feeding tubes in the same way as these other treatments, isn't it? I think that is because everyone agrees that feeding is a basic act of human caring. That is why the bishops want us to be especially careful in scrutinizing the context of the patient and the patient's benefits. The bishops seem to be wary of those who are too ready to stop medically assisted feeding for personal or social convenience. For example, what if this became a routine action? It could reflect a callous indifference that would infect the medical community and society at large.

So the bishops write, "There should be a presumption in favor of providing nutrition and hydration to all patients, including patients who require medically assisted nutrition and hydration, as long as this is of sufficient benefit to outweigh the burdens involved to the patient" (*ERD*, n. 58). Their qualification of "presumption" means that we would normally want to provide nutrition. The presumption in its favor resists callous indifference. But their calling for an assessment of benefits over burdens admits that, in some instances, patients might be artificially fed in ways that would be more harmful than helpful. It would be wrong to override the presumption without serious reasons and unless absolutely necessary. Where there is doubt, we ought to choose in favor of sustaining life further.

Mary, this is precisely where you feel the burden of this decision. Are the reasons sufficiently serious? Is it absolutely necessary? You will have to judge whether this proposed treatment will bring more benefits than burdens to John considered holistically, not just physically.

MARY: I know that if I refuse this treatment for John, he will surely die. What worries me more than anything is that I would be responsible for killing him.

PC: Yes, that is a heavy concern. Sometimes it is hard to distinguish between killing and allowing to die. I don't hear in you any intention to kill John. What I hear is that you want to stop what seems to be pointless treatment. But you do seem confused as to whether you would be the cause of his death by not allowing this treatment. Granted, there is a fine line to walk here.

In cases similar to John's, physicians have judged that it is the overall condition that makes patients choke when fed by mouth and miserable when fed by tubes. Were it not for medicine's ability to get around his

inability to take food by mouth, John would have died
months ago. The question before you is whether John's
inevitable death from an irreversible condition must be
resisted. Do you have an obligation to oppose those
physical conditions that make it impossible for John to
eat? If they go unopposed, then John's physical condition will be the cause of his death. I don't think that we
can conclude that you will be culpable for his death.

MARY: What I understand you to be saying, then, is that,
even though the required use of feeding tubes remains a
debated issue, I may be on reasonable grounds to refuse
this treatment for John, that the Catholic moral tradition
upholds weighing benefits and burdens from John's perspective to the extent that I can, and that I would not be
responsible for his death. That all seems to make sense to
me, but it is still hard emotionally. I am going to have to
sit with this a little while longer. But at least now I have a
clearer picture of the church's guidance in this matter and
of the moral dimensions of this case. Thank you.

Conclusion

Hard choices like Mary's require consultation and dialogue.
Values and disvalues must be identified and selected, responsibilities clarified, distinctions made, questions clarified, information
obtained, different perspectives tested. It is possible that someone
else may draw a different conclusion from Mary's. In a tough
case like this, even opposing decisions may be responsible. But
responsible decisions are what we seek. The task of the pastoral
minister is to guide the process of such decisions at the subjective
level to conform as much as possible to the objective truth, as
much as this can be known through inquiry and reason. If the pastoral minister has made a sincere effort to understand those seeking guidance, has encouraged them to seek the truth, and has
challenged them with objective teaching by presenting it as

clearly and sympathetically as possible, then the pastoral minister has served well as a moral guide. We can ask no more. If persons seeking guidance decide in a way other than we would, we must be able to honor their freedom of conscience, unless serious harm will result to themselves or others. Upholding the dignity of an informed conscience demands no less. In the end, each of us is bound to live and to stand by our own discernment of what God is asking of us in this moment. We must step into the future based on decisions made before God in the recesses of our own heart.

CRITICAL REFLECTION:

1. How does the above presentation on pastoral moral guidance affirm your present approach to this aspect of pastoral ministry? *I relearned that...*
2. What new insight did you gain from this chapter? *I was surprised to learn that...*
3. What questions does your new learning raise for you? *I need to think more about...*

APPROPRIATION:

1. Share an anecdote from your life that illustrates how you have offered or received moral guidance. *I remember when...*
2. How would you like to offer or receive moral guidance in the future? *Next time, I want to...*

Notes

1. CONSCIENCE

1. For a succinct treatment of the Freudian model of the person, see the still valuable article by George Zilboorg, "Superego and Conscience," in *Conscience: Theological and Psychological Perspectives,* ed. C. Ellis Nelson (New York: Newman Press, 1973), pp. 210–23.

2. John W. Glaser, "Conscience and Superego: A Key Distinction," in *Conscience,* pp. 167–88; first printed in *Theological Studies* 32 (March 1971): 30–47.

3. For a still valuable review of the ways that the tradition has talked about conscience, see Bernard Haring, *The Law of Christ,* vol. 1, *General Moral Theology,* trans. Edwin G. Kaiser (Paramus: Newman Press, 1966), pp. 135–89. Also, Bernard Haring, *Free and Faithful in Christ,* vol. 1, *General Moral Theology* (New York: Seabury Press, 1978), pp. 224–301.

4. Hans Walter Wolff, *Anthropology of the Old Testament* (Philadelphia: Fortress Press, 1974), pp. 40–55.

5. Robert Bolt, *A Man for All Seasons* (New York: Vintage Books, 1962), p. 81.

6. Joseph Allegretti, "A Person of Character," *Health Progress* 71 (April 1990): 88.

7. Martin Buber, *The Way of Man According to the Teaching of Hasidism* (New York: Citadel Press, 1966), p. 17.

8. Bolt, *A Man for All Seasons,* pp. 76–77.

9. Ken Kesey, *One Flew over the Cuckoo's Nest* (New York: New American Library, 1962), p. 126.

10. Viktor Frankl, *Man's Search for Meaning,* trans. Ilse Lasch, rev. ed. (New York: Simon and Schuster, 1962), p. 65.

11. Daniel C. Maguire has contributed significantly to understanding the affective dimension of morality; see especially his *The Moral Choice* (Garden City, NY: Doubleday, 1978), pp. 71–75, 84–86, 263–67, 281–305.

12. For a review of this research, see Sidney Callahan, *In Good Conscience* (New York: HarperCollins, 1991), pp. 186–90. See also Charles M. Shelton, *Morality of the Heart* (New York: Crossroad, 1990), pp. 33–59.

13. Mark Twain, *The Adventures of Huckleberry Finn,* p. 206.

2. Practical Reasoning

1. For a good overview of the notion of discernment as it pertains to the moral and spiritual life, see Mark O'Keefe, *Becoming Good, Becoming Holy* (New York: Paulist Press, 1995), pp. 125–44.

2. This method is inspired by the work of Sidney Callahan, *In Good Conscience.*

3. Social Context

1. The influence of communities on one's character and action has been a consistent concern of Stanley Hauerwas. See especially his *A Community of Character* (Notre Dame: University of Notre Dame Press, 1981). This theme has also been developed with a particular feminist interest in Gloria Albrecht, *The Character of Our Communities* (Nashville: Abingdon Press, 1995).

2. For this distinction between "revealed morality" and "revealed reality" in the Bible, I am following James M. Gustafson, "The Place of Scripture in Christian Ethics: A Methodological Study," in *Theology and Christian Ethics*

(Philadelphia: United Church Press, 1974), pp. 121–45, esp. pp. 129–38.

3. For an overview of the use of the Bible in ethics, see William C. Spohn, *What Are They Saying About Scripture and Ethics?* rev. ed. (New York: Paulist Press, 1995).

4. For a critical interpretation of the commandments, see Raymond F. Collins, *Christian Morality: Biblical Foundations* (Notre Dame, IN: University of Notre Dame Press, 1986), pp. 49–63.

5. A good example of this way of using scripture in ethics can be found in the U.S. bishops' pastoral letter, *Economic Justice for All* (Washington, DC: USCC, 1986), pp. 16–32.

6. For three perspectives on Jesus and the moral life, see James M. Gustafson, *Christ and the Moral Life* (New York: Harper and Row, 1968); Stanley Hauerwas, *The Peaceable Kingdom* (Notre Dame, IN: University of Notre Dame Press, 1983); and William C. Spohn, *What Are They Saying About Scripture and Ethics?* rev. ed. (New York: Paulist Press, 1995), pp. 94–102.

7. On this interpretation of Jesus in the moral life, see Spohn, *What Are They Saying About Scripture and Ethics?* p. 100.

8. For a valuable interpretation of the magisterium as moral teacher, see Francis A. Sullivan, *Magisterium: Teaching Authority in the Catholic Church* (New York: Paulist Press, 1983). A book of related interest on interpreting the degree of authority of magisterial documents is his *Creative Fidelity* (New York: Paulist Press, 1996).

9. On the importance of friendship in the moral life, see Paul J. Wadell, *Friendship and the Moral Life* (Notre Dame, IN: University of Notre Dame Press, 1989).

10. William J. Bennett, *Book of Virtues* (New York: Simon and Schuster, 1993).

11. The literature on the meaning and use of principles in ethics is vast. For an overview of what is at stake in this issue, see

my still useful book, *What Are They Saying About Moral Norms?* (New York: Paulist Press, 1981). For a more recent overview of the debate on principles as it pertains to bioethics, see Edwin R. DuBose, Ron Hamel, and Laurence J. O'Connell, eds., *A Matter of Principles?* (Valley Forge, PA: Trinity Press International, 1994).

4. SITUATIONAL CONTEXT

1. For an extended treatment of the reality-revealing questions, see Daniel C. Maguire, *The Moral Choice* (Garden City, NY: Doubleday, 1978), pp. 128–88.

5. PERSONAL CONTEXT

1. The emphasis on character and virtue in ethics has been getting a great deal of attention of late. Stanley Hauerwas is generally recognized as the theologian who has contributed significantly to the renewed interest in it. See especially his early major work on this subject, *Character and the Christian Life: A Study of Theological Ethics* (San Antonio, TX: Trinity University Press, 1975).

2. As found in Laura Schlessinger, *How Could You Do That?* (New York: HarperCollins, 1996), p. 23.

3. On the significance of emotion and intuition, I am indebted to the work of Sidney Callahan, especially *In Good Conscience* (New York: HarperCollins, 1991).

4. For an example of how religious beliefs influence the moral life, see James M. Gustafson, *Can Ethics Be Christian?* (Chicago: University of Chicago Press, 1975), pp. 48–116.

5. For a sustained treatment of the imagination in the moral life, see Philip S. Keane, *Christian Ethics and Imagination* (New York: Paulist Press, 1984).

6. For other images related to some of our leading moral issues, see *Ibid,* especially chapter 5, pp. 110–146.

7. For a succinct treatment of the role of prayer in the moral life, see Mark O'Keefe, *Becoming Good, Becoming Holy* (New York: Paulist Press, 1995), pp. 113–24.

6. Pastoral Moral Guidance

1. Bernard Haring, *Free and Faithful in Christ,* vol. 1, *General Moral Theology* (New York: Seabury Press, 1978), p. 289.